For Mrs. Anona _____,

who is imbued with the
basic principle of the
"Magna Carta — that
"government itself is
subject to law."

From Agnes Bowe

January 26, 1972

# Magna Carta

# Magna Carta

by

William F. Swindler

Illustrated by Mitchell Hooks

GROSSET & DUNLAP
PUBLISHERS    NEW YORK

*To*
*Our Children*
*Betty and Bill*

# Contents

# 1

# The King
# and the Barons

A GAME of chess, played with armed men for deadly stakes, appeared to be moving toward checkmate on a certain Monday in June in the year 1215. The black king of England had lost most of his protecting pawns, and there seemed to be only a few moves left before his remaining pieces would also be taken. With his opponent in control of the board, what could the king then do but admit that he had lost the game?

Loyalties were loosely held in the Middle Ages. King John was not the first or the last monarch to discover that when the fortunes of the crown were in decline, a king's subjects could find any number of reasons for deserting him. A sovereign's faults were often real enough—promises unkept, the levying of unfair taxes, justice unevenly administered, and the failure to revenge attack on those he was sworn to defend. But when the king was at the height of his power, the wise subject kept his peace and waited. Time could bring change or it could weaken the ruler and lay him open to revolt.

After seventeen years on the throne, King John could well claim that England as a kingdom had fared better with him than it had under the reign of his brother, Richard the Lion Heart. That popular, dashing figure had spent most of his ten-year rule abroad fighting a Crusade against the non-Christian infidels who controlled the Holy Land, sacred birthplace of Jesus Christ. To confound matters further, Richard, on returning from the wars, had allowed himself to be captured by robber barons and held for ransom. The money paid for his release had almost bankrupted England. Still, John had reason to be grateful for his brother's long absence, during which he had plotted actively to seize his throne—just as he and Richard together had plotted to destroy their father, King Henry II.

Medieval life in England was, indeed, a game of chess played by the great lords of the realm; the advantage kept shifting, and when men guessed who the winner would ultimately be, they moved frantically to get to his side. A strong and able king, or at least a lucky one, could keep the advantage—and hence the loyalty of his vassals—throughout his reign; a weak, inept or unlucky ruler could expect to have his followers turn against him. King Henry II, until the tragic last months of his life, had been strong and able; Richard had been lucky; and John had not possessed any of these qualities.

The medieval way of life made law and order almost meaningless. Over the centuries, from the fall of Rome to the coming of the modern age, men had tried to find a formula for stable government but had not succeeded. The kind of central authority exercised by the Roman Empire, and the guarantees of justice set down in Roman law, had not existed for more than seven hundred years. Medieval Europe was a map of continually changing small duchies, warring kingdoms, isolated walled cities, secluded monasteries, provinces and principalities over which hereditary claimants constantly clashed.

To achieve some kind of order in medieval society, a system gradually grew up in Europe that we later called feudalism. Oddly enough, it was in England, a small compact island isolated from the rest of the European continent, that feudalism proved most successful. There, under the Norman and Angevin dynasties, whose rule ran successively for several hundred years, the feudal structure took root and became more firmly established than anywhere else in the Western world. Endorsed by the Holy Roman Church, which had replaced the authority of the Roman Empire, feudal codes became the sole unifying force amid the turmoil and uncertainty of the lawless Middle Ages.

Feudalism was, essentially, a system based on an exchange of promises between the owners of land and their tenants. The lord of the land gave the tenant the use of his property, in return for which the tenant, or vassal, took an oath of fealty to the lord. The binding moral force of this vow upon those who took it was the power of the Church to visit damnation on its violators. In an age when belief was strong, both in God and in miracles, this oath, presumably, was neither lightly taken nor lightly broken. The tenant also acquired, in exchange for his promise of loyalty, the lord's guarantee, or warranty, of the tenant's estate rights in the land he received from the lord. This was a most important part of the arrangement, for the possession of land during these troubled times was deemed to be the most effective source of security and power. Consequently, it was land itself—real, visible and seemingly permanent—that became the highest measure of value in medieval life. The great nobles, or overlords—with the king as first lord of the realm—expected their vassals to maintain themselves in military readiness, together with as many armed retainers as their land would support, should the lord require their services in battle. A tenant's duty to help his lord in combat—known as knight's service—was another of the obligations he assumed as a vassal.

One can picture the feudal system as a pyramid, with the king at the top. Directly under him were the greatest barons called the lords temporal, and the bishops, or the lords spiritual. Because they held their lands and other "tenements" on a grant from the crown, they were usually called crown tenants or tenants in chief. While feudalism flourished, there were seldom more than two hundred of these great lords in the realm; but their land holdings were vast and therefore they owed much to the crown. For their own security, the crown tenants would pass much of this burden on to their own vassals. They divided up their land among the lesser lords, whose power was roughly midway, or *mesne,* in the feudal ranks.

The first loyalty of these mesne lords was to the crown tenants and not to the crown itself. Mesne lords, in turn, also could divide their holdings among men who owed everything, including their loyalty, to them. The tenants under the mesne lords, called tenants paravail, were at the base of the pyramid. Each lord in the rank—the king, the tenants in chief, the mesne lords and the tenants paravail—had his own holdings. Each had produce and services owed directly to him by those beneath him. And each also had his own castles, villages, farms, woodlands or forests, religious houses and people.

The England of John's day—and even the England of William the Conqueror a century and a half earlier—was a fairly civilized society, but the lifelong obligations that were inherited with one's station in life made it a restless one. Many continually tried to evade obligations they thought unfair or unendurable. Many tried to make harsher demands upon men below them in the hierarchy. In the course of time, groups or localities forced special concessions from their overlords or won back rights lost under the feudal system. Thus, independent towns or boroughs, and some manors or ecclesiastical houses, gained charters freeing them from the regular obligations of the system.

This was England in the heart of the Middle Ages. Some two million persons lived under the rule of a handful of lords in a system of landholding that had been developing since the Normans had invaded and conquered England. The Normans' defeat of the ruling Saxons at Hastings in 1066 had been a turning point in English as well as world history. The Normans had brought with them the seed of an idea of central government that had almost died with the Roman Empire. In English soil the seed took root, and over generations it flourished.

William was the French Duke of Normandy and Conqueror of England, Scotland, Wales and Ireland (although not even William could truly subdue the fierce Irish Celts). In England, he was the father of feudalism. Saxon life had been simple; villages were fairly independent of one another, and the king's power had fallen into decline. William's new ways of organizing power and property soon won out over the old customs. William took over all the lands of England and then granted them back to his tenants in chief as a reward for services. Since all land now came from the crown, a tenant "held" his land rather than owned it. The king's power to rule and govern was enormously increased, for the vassal who dared to be disloyal could be stripped of his estate if the crown so desired.

William I had spent his youth putting down rebellious tenants throughout Normandy. He spent his twenty years in England after the Conquest doing the same thing. He was a ferocious fighter, a firm ruler and a farsighted administrator who laid a solid foundation for English feudalism. Despite the rise and fall of many kings, feudalism would survive for generations to come. To strengthen the control of his realm, William built a series of royal fortresses, the greatest of which was the Tower of London. To make sure his subjects would not forget their obligation to the crown, he compelled all tenants to swear the Oath of Salisbury to renew their loyalty to him. So that he might assess all the resources of the kingdom, he called for the first great census. This record became known as the Domesday Book.

At William's death, certain events showed both how strong and how weak was the kingdom that stretched from Brittany in France to Scotland. He left Normandy and the other French holdings to his eldest son, Robert, and to his second son, William—sometimes called Rufus because of his ruddy complexion —he left England. Henry, the youngest son, who received only

money as his inheritance, watched and waited. He was ready
to pounce at a misstep by either brother and seize the throne for
himself. But the first question was, to which monarch—the King
of England or the Duke of Normandy—were the lords of the
realm to give their homage and loyalty?

Legally, a vassal was bound to swear loyalty to the lord who
owned his estate. But often one tenant owed obligations to
several lords, each of whose lands he held by separate vow. The
barons who had followed William I to England had obligations
to him both for their ancient lands in Normandy and for their
new estates in England that had been granted them as rewards
for their support in the Conquest. Now, therefore, the barons
had divided loyalties. In Rouen, the great stronghold in Normandy, they paid homage to Duke Robert, and in England they
renewed their feudal vows for their English estates with William II.

This conflict led to a practical problem. In a battle between
the king and the duke, how would the crown tenants fulfill
their obligations of men and arms? If they supported one lord,
would not the other call them traitors and strip them of the
estates they held of him? This same conflict of interest pre-
vailed at all levels of the feudal system. Thus, many a tenant,
when his lords were at odds, would have to renounce his oath
to one and throw in his lot with the other. It also explained
why medieval kings, after subduing rebellious tenants, would
take them back as followers if they renewed their oaths of
loyalty. It was commonly recognized and accepted that, in any
test of power, loyalty would go to the overlord who seemed most
likely to win.

The struggle of Robert against William II threatened the
kingdom William the Conqueror had created. But the issue
was finally settled by an agreement between the brothers. In
exchange for funds to equip an army for the Crusades, Robert
ceded formal control of Normandy to William. The two thrones
were thus reunited under one ruler. Now only one brother and

one throne stood between Henry, the Conqueror's youngest son, and his kingly ambitions. In the year 1100, William II was killed in what appeared to be a hunting accident. Some voiced suspicion about the part played by brother Henry in this so-called accident. But the murmurings ceased when Henry moved swiftly and took over the throne.

Neither William II nor Henry I had their father's administrative abilities. But they meted out justice as they understood it. More importantly, they knew how to employ military force rapidly and effectively, and thus kept the lords of the realm in relative obedience throughout the Norman period. Upon assuming the throne, Henry added one new feature to the kingly rites, which had importance for the future of feudalism. In the manner of the old Saxon kings, he took a coronation oath that acknowledged certain responsibilities to be borne by an English monarch. First, the very fact that he took an oath was itself an admission that a king had obligations toward his subjects. Secondly, the oath admitted that the feudal system itself required periodic reform to correct injustices and other abuses, such as those that had sprung up under the rule of William II.

Lords had had to pay huge fees or reliefs for the right to inherit their estates; widows and daughters of tenants had been forced into marriages at the command of their overlords; church positions had been left vacant for long periods so that the revenues which would have gone to the parish, abbey or cathedral went to the crown or to the crown tenant who was the "lord of the fee." A century later, when John's vassals held up Henry's oath as a precedent to be used against their king, the same abuses were still part of English life.

Under strong kings, however, the feudal system was workable. The types of tenants gradually became more varied. Some lords held their fees or fiefs by serving as knights in the king's army. Among the lowest ranks of tenants were those who held their lands by *socage,* an arrangement that enabled them to work as free farmers who paid their fees in agricultural produce. As for the tenants connected with the church, they took over the responsibilities of charity called *frankalmoin* (literally, "free alms"), which relieved the crown and barons of caring for the poor and the sick. It became more expensive to keep armies beyond the needs for local protection, and many tenants paid *scutages* ("shield money") so that the overlord could hire professional fighting men.

Henry defeated his eldest brother, Robert, who had laid claim to the crowns of Normandy and England on his return from the First Crusade. As he established his authority, King Henry introduced the beginnings of official positions that one day would develop into a national government. A treasurer took care of the royal revenues. Overseeing of crown properties throughout the land became the responsibility of a chancellor. A justiciar—the realm's chief judicial officer—acted as Henry's deputy in England while he attended to the affairs of state in Normandy. These and other close advisers were the king's court, and rode with him as he continually traveled about his kingdom; a single capital city for all of England was still in the future. When the king wished to hold "deep speech" with all of the great lords of the realm, he would summon them to a council wherever he intended to be; a regular Parliament was still a century and a half distant.

These steps toward an ever stronger central government were feared by the crown tenants. The barons would let the King take the role of *primus inter pares*—first among equals—but they were determined at all times to preserve their own rights and rule over their lands. Strong monarchs threatened the self-interests of the barons, who were always alert for a chance to bring the throne under their domination. Under William I and his two sons, however, the opportunity never arose.

When Henry I died in 1135, the chance seemed to have come at last. The king had died without a male heir. His only legitimate daughter Matilda, or Maud, had married Geoffrey of Anjou, a noble house traditionally hostile to Normans. The barons tried to take advantage of a not uncommon problem in the history of medieval monarchies: when more than one person claimed the throne, who should be king? For often no claimant could prove he was the legal heir. In this case, the barons had sworn to Henry that they would accept Matilda. Now they argued that her marriage to a hostile foreign ruler freed them from their oath; and Matilda's son was an unlikely candidate because he was two generations removed from the late king.

Candidates in the natural order of succeeding generations were available, however, in the sons of Henry's sister Adela. Since the sons were not in a direct line of descent from Henry, the way was open for bargaining between the barons and the claimants. The way was also open for an opportunist. And while deliberations over the succession were still in progress, Adela's younger son Stephen suddenly appeared in London and appealed to the people of the city to proclaim him king. Under an ancient, if vague right held by their city, the Londoners did so; Stephen was anointed and crowned before the barons could prevent it. His uncle, Henry I, who had won his own crown by keeping an eye open for the big chance, might have chuckled in his tomb had the joke not been on himself, his daughter and his grandson.

The stormy reign of the last of the Normans demonstrated many things about feudalism. There was a basic self-seeking and savagery under the thin surface of order. And feudalism depended on a powerful, and sometimes ruthless overlord for effective enforcement of order. Most importantly, it was a constant invitation to a division of loyalties. Stephen was the worst of all possible kings in such a system—an indecisive though well-meaning man whose commands were bound to be ignored. Within half a dozen years he had been deposed by his cousin

Matilda, who invaded England seeking the throne. Stephen regained the throne shortly thereafter, by agreeing to name Matilda's son Henry as his heir. During the eight years remaining of Stephen's reign, his realm was ravaged at will by rival lords who had once been held in check.

The Norman period had been at its peak under William I and Henry I. Now the Angevins (from Anjou), or the Plantagenets,* as they were called, would begin a new era in feudal history. Their rule commenced with a king as brilliant and successful as William the Conqueror. Henry II, like his grandfather, advanced the growth of government institutions significantly in the thirty-five years of his reign.

His first problem was to control the barons who had been rebellious under Stephen. Henry made it clear that feudal obligations would be renewed and enforced, and, to see that they were, he soon began to send out his own circuit judges to administer royal justice throughout England. Thus were planted the seeds of a uniform or common law. Henry and his great justiciar, Ranulph de Glanville, created important new legal procedures for coping with the major concerns of feudalism, landholding and its obligations. And to make sure these procedures worked, Henry took over the jurisdiction of the law from baronial courts.

The procedures, called by their Norman French names, dealt with problems of feudal tenancies: landlords absent from their holdings, short life expectancies and disputed inheritances, and the material or economic problems of land held by the church. The first assize, or subject of the court session, dealt with a common difficulty called *novel disseisin,* or recent dispossession. In the course of periodic visits to his scattered holdings, a tenant might find that a rival had moved onto his

* The name is said to have come from the family's practice of *planting* the *genista* (broom plant) to make hunting shelters.

land. If the tenant did not challenge him, the invader might feel free to make a claim to the title of the estate. Three courses of action were open to the injured claimant. He could first try on the spot to throw out the intruder. Trial by battle, a slightly more formal form of violence, was also an old Norman custom. Or he could make a complaint of *novel disseisin* in the royal courts. The last choice was quickly found to be so effective that it displaced the cruder methods. And often it became a way to test a disputed title to land, whether there had been actual dispossession or not.

The second assize of *mort d'ancestor* also had its roots in familiar experience: upon the death (*mort*) of an "ancestor" (parent, relative, or guardian) the successor to an estate would find that a rival was claiming the estate as the rightful heir. The sheriff (from the Saxon *shire-reeve*) was the King's chief officer in a county or shire; the assize gave him power to determine whether the "ancestor" lawfully owned the estate at the time of his death. If so, the claimant was the rightful heir.

The final assize of *darrein presentment* involved the feudal right of "presentment" of a candidate for a vacancy in an office of the church. This was the right of the tenant who had founded the particular church or religious house. If some rival had taken the vacancy for his own candidate, the tenant could now seek justice from the King, as the one who had made the last (*darrein*) rightful presentment.

Under this new system of justice, enforced by the royal judges with their armed retinue, Henry II accounted for an effective "modernization" of feudal law. Glanville, or his associates using his name, prepared a record of English common law as it was now understood and practiced, and before the end of the century the royal courts began to keep rolls of manuscripts of decrees and decisions, charters and records of payments of fees.

Criminal law, which was concerned with offenses against the king's peace, now became the exclusive business of the royal courts. Whether the subject was a criminal complaint or the crown's claim against a tenant, a specialized section of the courts now heard pleas (formal proceedings) of the crown. Proceedings between tenants, called common pleas, soon began to be heard regularly in courts situated near Westminster, where the records were available. So Henry's court system hastened the day when a rule of law throughout England would become possible.

Under Henry II, the first Plantagenet, the realm prospered and grew powerful. By his marriage to Eleanor of Aquitaine, Henry added a vast, rich province to the south of the Angevin possessions in Europe. England held its own island, plus a large section of Europe that stretched to the Pyrenees Mountains at the border of what is now Spain. England was by far the most powerful kingdom in Christendom. At the midpoint in Henry's reign, it seemed that she had all but reached a golden age.

But progress could be made only up to a point. New concepts of law and order had to take root and grow. And the barons, who had been so firmly curbed by the King's strong arm, were growing restless again. The Plantagenets were known for their monumentally bad tempers, which did not endear them to anyone. They weren't used to seeking compromises with equally stubborn forces. Henry started a violent conflict with the Church when he reasserted royal judicial authority over matters that had been considered the province of church law. One tragic result of this historic conflict was the exile and assassination of the great Archbishop of Canterbury, Thomas à Becket.

An empire as great as Henry's provoked jealousies abroad. The French kingdom centered around Paris was bitterly resentful because Henry had married Eleanor. She had been betrothed to their own indolent Louis, and the marriage would

have given France the balance of power in European politics. Eleanor herself retained the homage of the lords of Aquitaine. She continued her own court there in virtual defiance of her husband and trained her sons to seek their own advantages in the never-ending power struggle of medieval court life and politics.

Tragedy lay ahead of Henry in his last years. His son Richard was next in the line of succession to his crown. But Henry regarded Richard, who was Eleanor's favorite, as his enemy. Thus, there was only John, his remaining son, to whom he could turn as a confidant and ally in this final bitter period of his reign. Everywhere he looked, the old king found himself hemmed in. His household was riddled with opposing ambitions. The barons of his realm could no longer be counted upon for their loyal support. And jealous foes abroad menaced the empire he sought to hold together and maintain even as the power slipped from his hands.

The story behind King John's accession to the throne is a tale of unending rivalries set against a dark background of plot and counterplot. Richard, who was well aware of his father's preference for John, feared that he might be cheated out of the throne. So he listened eagerly when Philip, the new King of France, outlined a plot to overthrow Henry. John also joined the plotters, reasoning that his father's removal would bring him one step closer to the crown. And Eleanor, too, did her part by weakening Henry's hold on his French possessions. The king had imprisoned her in an attempt to stop her intrigues, but Eleanor still managed to communicate with her loyal nobles in Aquitaine and through them to fan the flames of opposition to Henry in Brittany and Anjou.

In this atmosphere of conspiracy, the great King Henry came to a humiliating end, deserted by almost all of his followers and trapped by the combined forces of Philip and his own sons. Racked with fever and broken in spirit, Henry, the first of the Plantagenets, died in Normandy in the year 1188, far from the scene of his great works in England.

But Richard, who had wanted the power of the throne at any price, had none of his father's interest in the responsibilities of government. He had already "taken the cross"— vowed to embark on a Crusade—and the great adventure that this promised was for him far more exciting than the work of restoring order to an empire that had been torn apart by his own conspiring.

For the next ten years, England and Normandy were ruled by an absentee monarch. After Richard's coronation, six years elapsed before he again set foot on the island. England, during this period, was governed by a loyal and able regency under Archbishop Hubert Walter of Canterbury, Archbishop Walter de Coutances of Rouen and the Earl of Pembroke, William Marshal. Richard's long absence began the decline of the empire in Normandy, as Philip of France worked ceaselessly to weaken the ties with the English crown. And at home John's own ambition for the throne provided another threat.

John tried to seize power when he heard that Richard had been captured in Austria by robber barons. But the revolt came to an end with news of Richard's release. People in the Middle Ages, who respected military power, were always ready to rally to a natural warrior like Richard the Lion Heart. John's opportunity came at last in the late winter of 1199 when the king was fatally wounded by an arrow during an expedition in France.

Even then, John's claim to the crown was disputed. Richard, still devoted to his mother's cause in Aquitaine, had proposed his nephew Arthur as his successor, and the King of France had eagerly supported the candidacy. John managed to thwart the efforts of both Philip and Arthur to defeat him in battle. Putting to rout a force commanded by Arthur, he captured its leaders, including his nephew. He also secured the treasuries at Rouen and Winchester and was crowned Duke of Normandy and King of England. With Arthur in his power, the threat to John was lessened. But the king could not rest easy while his nephew lived. The royal prisoner was secretly put to death, strangled, it is said, by John himself.

John, by the brutal standards of the early thirteenth century, was not a wicked king—only an inept one. The moral issue of arranging Arthur's death was less important than the unwise policy behind it. Arthur as a living hostage would have allowed him to negotiate with Philip and to keep the reluctant support of Anjou and Aquitaine—while Arthur dead gave both of these provinces an excuse for defecting to France. It also gave Philip an excuse for a punitive invasion of Normandy. Moreover, John had been guilty of an even more dangerous error—he had failed to see that a fundamental change in the feudal order had taken place in the century and a half since the Conquest. The men who had followed William I from Normandy to England had been given estates in both realms; but in the generations that had followed, as their French holdings kept being divided, the majority of their descendants—most of the great barons in England—no longer had personal holdings on the Continent. They had become Englishmen, with no particular desire to fight John's battles in a land across the Channel.

Although the English lords gave their king little support in his effort to hold the old Norman empire together, they did not hesitate to blame him for its loss. To John, the behavior of his English vassals was treasonable, and when Philip drove him back across the Channel he was determined to put an end to this intolerable denial of his rights as first lord of the realm.

John's return marked the beginning of a decade of conflict. Suspicious of all around him—usually with good cause—the king was determined to protect his realm from all foreign influences. When Archbishop Walter died, John tried to choose his successor. But a group of churchmen at Canterbury also claimed this privilege. The issue was left to Pope Innocent in Rome. Would he decide on John's candidate, or would he rule in favor of the churchmen?

Innocent tried to settle the dispute by what he thought was a clever compromise. Instead of picking one of the rival candidates, he chose a third party for the post. The new Archbishop was Stephen Langton, a patriot and scholar whose selection was to have historic consequences for the rule of law in England. Ordinarily, John might not have objected to Innocent's action. But this was a clear case of his royal wish being flouted. His anger aroused, John lodged a strong protest with the pope. When Innocent paid no attention and consecrated Langton in Rome, John struck back. Langton was not permitted to land in England; and the vengeful John also seized the properties of the offending churchmen at Canterbury.

The pope, however, could also play this game. In retaliation, he forbade the sacraments of baptism, marriage or burial to any English subject until John yielded. When this move failed to budge the king, Innocent excommunicated him. Thus, the contest between pope and monarch, which had gone on for several years, came to a dramatic climax in the year 1208.

But John was less afraid of the pope's spiritual powers than of his political and military might. He was quick to see a practical danger: Innocent might send a formal papal commission to a European prince—with Philip of France as the most obvious prospect. This commission would encourage Philip to invade England in the name of the Holy Church and depose the king. John knew when he was outmaneuvered, and prepared to convert the situation to his advantage. He sent word that he was prepared for a reconciliation, welcomed Archbishop Langton to England, surrendered his crown to the papal legate and Innocent granted it back to him as a fief of the Holy See.

Now the king was clothed with the investiture of the church itself, which acted as a deterrent to further plots of rebellion by the crown tenants. Yet John's capacity for courting new disasters after averting present ones had not been exhausted. Now that England again seemed under control, he launched upon a desperate and ill-conceived plan to recapture England's lost possessions in France. The campaign ended in defeat. John finally signed a treaty that surrendered the major part of the Continental holdings of the Norman-Angevin succession. Then he returned to face dissension and a new restlessness at home.

The stage was now set for the events drawing John to a meadow near the Thames called Runnymede. John's own conduct led him to that spot: where Henry II had ruled by firmness, John ruled by violence, and where Richard I had benefited from the wisdom of capable regents, John abused and ignored the few men of principle who could be found in this turbulent age. But his enemies were no better; most of the conspirators gathered for the final challenge to royal authority wanted only to restore the reign of freebooting that their grandfathers had enjoyed under Stephen.

This time, however, a different Stephen stood in the way of anarchy—Stephen Langton, Innocent's appointee to the See of Canterbury. It was now June, 1215, and the archbishop was the only man in the land who could mediate between the king and the angry forces opposing him. As the rival camps poised for battle, it was Langton who proposed the compromise settlement that made history—a charter for an orderly society that feudalism had thus far sought in vain.

# 2

# The Great Charter

IN the forty years between the death of Henry II and the coming of age of Henry III, two men of high principle stood out conspicuously.

One was Archbishop Langton. Although he was born in England, he grew up and was educated in Paris, a doctor of theology at the university. Innocent summoned him to Rome in 1206 to become a cardinal-priest of the Church of St. Chrysogomus. He knew Philip of France well and was a respected member of the papal college. But, most important, he was recognized in his own time as the greatest English-born cleric of the age. Langton held no grudge against John for the years the king had kept him from the throne of Canterbury. He saw his duty clearly: together, he and King John shared the responsibility for the Church and the state of England, and this heavy duty left no room for personal quarrels.

But John's feelings were not so noble. When Langton softened the demands of the barons and reduced them to the great principles of the charter, the king denounced the archbishop to the pope and secured a relief from the charter's obligations in a matter of weeks. John insisted upon the absolute powers of the crown; Langton thought of its responsibilities.

The other great man of the time was William Marshal, the

31

Earl of Pembroke. In his own life he showed the steadfast loyalty that was the mark of feudalism at its best. He served four kings well and truly—Henry I, each of his sons, and his grandson. Richard the Lion Heart, who had plotted against Henry, nonetheless admired the brave man who stood by the king in his final betrayal. In fact, Richard gave him the hand of the heiress of Pembroke. This marriage brought Marshal one of the greatest estates in England. Like Langton, the earl remained on John's side in the crisis of 1215. He was less interested in increasing the powers of the crown than in protecting the realm against the rapacity of the barons. After John died, he would be the faithful protector of the minor Henry III until his own death.

Stephen Langton looked beyond the quarrels of his age, and inserted in the Great Charter principles that would guide the state for centuries. John would sign it reluctantly, and indeed would enlist even Innocent III's aid in taking back the rights he signed away, but Marshal would stand by the charter, and the charter would survive. Langton's genius drafted the charter; Marshal's sense of public welfare insured its reissue and preservation. Ten years after Runnymede, Henry III came of age and reissued the charter in its final form. By that time it had settled permanently into the framework of English law.

The problems between John and the barons might have resulted in only another set of promises to be forgotten when the crisis had passed. Instead, it was reaffirmed many times throughout the Middle Ages, revived in a modern understanding during the English Revolution of the seventeenth century, and then became the foundation for both English and American constitutional freedoms.

Langton, seeing that the barons and the king would soon openly oppose each other, searched the lessons of English history for a basic principle to which both sides could agree. And in August 1213, at a council at St. Albans, he presented to the assembled lords the document on which the principle could be based. It was a copy of the coronation charter of Henry I. It allowed the tenants to assert their rights against the crown— and to swear their loyalty in return.

The great lords were deeply impressed. Here was a charter of rights which showed that since the beginning of feudalism under the Normans the king had acknowledged his own duties to his people. The barons left St. Albans vowing to insist upon the basic guarantees of Henry's charter. Langton was smart enough to realize that they would rewrite this into a list of demands to their own advantage—as indeed they did. On the day of Epiphany in 1215, they served a list of forty-nine "articles" on the King.

Between that time and the final presentation of these demands after Easter that year, a mysterious document known as the Unknown Charter of Liberties happened to come to light. There were those who would mutter that Stephen Langton himself had written it, for it was a much milder document than the barons' Articles. Perhaps it was true, for no one could give a better account of where the Unknown Charter had come from. In any event, Stephen Langton would be the man to balance the selfish interests of the lords with some of the wording of the Unknown Charter.

A general uprising of the barons began in March. In the main, the rebels gathered in the east and north of England. If they were defeated, they could readily flee to Scotland or across the sea to Paris, where much of the plot had been hatched. The armies marched on the royal castles. They pushed their attack most strongly at Northampton. But John was ready for them. His fortresses were garrisoned and his troops were armed. Northampton held out against the invaders, and the royal forces were unable to mount a counterattack. The citizens of London joined forces with the barons and opened the city gates to the rebel army.

The king was now at a strategic disadvantage. Controlling London, the great mercantile center on the Thames, the rebels could offer a safe route for invasion from France, where Prince Louis was already assembling his armies. A French army on English soil might end in civil war. John knew he had to stall for time, and one way to do this was to come to an agreement with his crown tenants. The Articles of the Barons, as the archbishop read them to him, was close to an order for complete surrender. At this point John was ready to accept almost anything less harsh than the Articles. Langton saw this as an opportunity to draft his own comprehensive statement of the feudal law as all good men should observe it.

This was the prelude to the showdown at Runnymede. On Monday, June 15, John and his party rode to the meadow described as "between Staines and Winsor" on the south bank of the Thames. The chief rebels met them there—with an intervening force led by the Archbishop of Canterbury, the Archbishop of Dublin, and a group of the most influential bishops in the realm. After the event, hostile chroniclers pictured John almost as a fugitive brought to bay at this place, surrounded by righteously angry barons trying to prevent the king from destroying the land. The truth was that the parties of John and the barons appeared to be of equal strength—which again whetted Langton's hopes for a compromise.

As the two bodies of lords eyed each other tensely, belted for battle if the need arose, the Archbishop read, in sonorous Latin, the sixty-three propositions that had been drawn from both the Articles of the Barons and the Unknown Charter of Liberties. The wording of the barons' demands had been softened but in principle they were left nearly intact. They included all of the guarantees of Henry I, and a number of those that had become law under Henry II. These were all set down in the authoritative manuscript of Glanville and preserved in the rolls of laws at Westminster.

Thinking very different thoughts, all present listened intently. The king was already planning an appeal to Rome and the strengthening of his forces to the south and west; the rebel barons were disgruntled perhaps at the way their articles were edited but were glad that it was Langton who spoke for them. The churchmen and the citizens of London and other chartered boroughs were looking to preserve their own interests.

The document was a description of the obligations and services that fell upon every man in medieval life. Over the years, some details would become obsolete and eventually would be stricken from the rolls of laws. The wording of other details would remain, although the meaning might change with the times. But certain rights remain almost the same in the twentieth century as in the thirteenth.

The Charter reading opened with a lengthy introduction or preamble* which showed what parties were on hand: the archbishops and principal bishops of England and Ireland; the papal legate, Pandulph; and the head of the military religious order of the Knights Templar in England, Brother Aymeric— eleven churchmen in all, led by Stephen Langton. Then followed sixteen names of temporal lords, most of whom could be identified as John's party. The king must have had his northern borders securely in hand, and his last continental province behind him, for the list included the constable of Scotland, Alan of Galloway; and the steward of Poitou, Hubert de Burgh. Of all the persons named in the preamble, none were fully committed rebels. These were serious men here to make sure that the right promises were made and kept. The king's fiercest enemies feared his revenge, and managed to miss this meeting.

The Charter was addressed to all the lords, spiritual and temporal, and to all "justiciars, foresters, sheriffs, provosts, officers, and all his bailiffs" to whom the king would send copies. Thus, the whole range of feudal England was included. The details of the document show that even the humbler folk who

* See the translation of this text in the Appendix.

made up most of the population were taken into account. The meaning of this charter grew from a narrow compact between lords and tenants into a general statement of legal rights and responsibilities for all people.

The opening "chapter" following the preamble points out how broad were the aims of the Charter. The wording survives to the present—and in revised form appears in modern English statutes.

> . . . by this our present Charter we have confirmed, for us and our heirs forever, that the English Church shall be free, and shall have all her rights entire and her liberties inviolate. We have also granted to all freemen of our kingdom, for us and our heirs forever, all the underwritten liberties to be had and held by them and their heirs, of us and our heirs, forever.

To the men at Runnymede in 1215, the phrase "the English Church shall be free" meant that it was to be free from the crown's interference; to the men of the English Reformation, centuries later, it meant that the Church was to be free of control by the pope in Rome. To the lords and tenants of the thirteenth century, the term "freeman" meant a freeholder, a person who had rights to land under the feudal system. To the revolutionists of the seventeenth century, most men in England were freeholders. Today, it is taken to include all adult citizens.

After Langton opened the Charter with this general promise of liberty, he had to deal with the basic grievances the lords had tried to redress by bloodshed. The next seven chapters concerned the most pressing of these—the security of the land upon which all rights of feudalism were based. As in the days of Henry I, the uppermost problem was that of huge fees for the right to inherit property. The "relief" demanded by the overlord, the original grantor of the estate, was a payment by the heir for the right to take over the land after the previous tenant had died. The sum was in proportion to the importance of the estate—a hundred pounds for an earldom or a barony, a hundred shillings at most for a knight's fee.

Although these amounts had been established by "the ancient custom of the fees," lease grantors were always trying to get more money in the "relief." An heir who needed to take over his estate promptly would have to pay a high price rather than risk a long legal settlement. In other cases, a relief was demanded when an heir came of age. The guardian of a minor heir had use of the revenues from the young heir's estate. By feudal law the guardian was owed no more money at the time the estate passed back into the hands of its rightful heir.

The guardian was also expected to keep up the heir's property and not strip it of everything of value before turning it back. If the guardian was supposed to arrange a marriage for his ward, he shouldn't allow marriage beneath the ward's social station, which would "disparage" the estate. He could not force widows, who came under the protection of the lord of the estate, to remarry; and he had to see that they received their property.

Feudalism was built on loyalty and land, and the land, at all costs, was to be preserved. It must provide the resources in men or goods that it was expected to provide. Tenants— able-bodied men prepared for combat or capable of producing valuable provisions—were to be in control at all times. Minor heirs were to have their estates maintained by the guardians, and widows were to have their means of support insured. In this manner, the charter assured the security of tenants, minors, and women.

But not only the overlord despoiled the lands of tenants, wards or widows. The king and his officers were often just as unfair. So the next group of chapters took up the methods of the crown in the treatment of estates. When a man died in debt, the money he owed the king was the first to be paid from his property. But the royal treasury was almost always empty, and greedy kings would often seize a whole estate in payment for a very small debt. At times the crown would not take many pains to track down someone who owed it money, but would force payment from the nearest person who had backed up the debtor with a pledge. The charter sought to prohibit these practices.

When a person borrows money today or is in debt, he normally pays back the debt plus a percentage of the total amount, which is known as interest. The high interest on debts during the height of the Plantagenets was another point of protest. Under church law of the Middle Ages, Christians were forbidden to lend money at interest. As a consequence, those persons with no country, the European Jews, were the main source of loans. In England the crown was the protector of the moneylenders, who were often called "the King's Jews." From time to time, Plantagenet kings made money taking over the debt claims held by the Jews. They would force the debtors to pay and keep at least the interest rate for the royal treasury without violating the church law. Chapters on debt relief logically followed the chapter on debt claims in general.

This much of the Charter was hard enough for John to accept, but Chapter 13 must have roused his anger. Here was a demand from another group facing the king at Runnymede—the citizens of London and other free towns. These, the tradesmen and small businessmen, all the common people who lived in the towns without land of their own, had in the past no love for the great crown tenant, who often lived in great luxury from the labors of his vassals and the products of his estate. And both the landed gentry and the townspeople mistrusted the way the Church used its power. However, John's rule was so harsh that for the first time all people banded together as Englishmen rather than as social or economic classes. Only by winning over the townspeople and the lesser clergy had the barons been able to force the Charter upon King John. Unity for the first time put the people in a fair position to bargain. Now a king would often punish towns by demanding the surrender of their charters if he found the inhabitants plotting against him. Londoners, who had recently committed treason against the crown by welcoming the rebels, now wanted to be certain that their treachery would not be used to destroy charter rights that had been theirs long before the Conquest itself. John must have scowled as he read this escape clause for the townspeople.

The Charter then took up another abuse—the demanding of "aids," or special revenues for the overlord. By feudal law the overlord could ask for aids on only three occasions. These were the ransoming of the lord himself if he were kidnaped; the ceremonies (and expenses) of making his oldest son a knight; and the money to be raised when his oldest daughter was married. The tenants were expected to ransom their lord as often as he was unlucky enough to be captured. The other aids were to be a reasonable sum, and payable only once.

Some of the government functions the Charter wanted regularized. Thus, Chapter 17 stated that the court of "common pleas shall not follow our court, but be held in some place certain." It was common knowledge that the king's traveling judges were often open to bribes and corruption. A permanent court with records would be a safeguard for justice. The courts of common pleas would be most convenient near Westminster, where the records of past decisions, laws, charters, debts and other documents were on deposit. The Great Charter thus gave England its first permanent capital.

The Charter also guaranteed that tenants could recover lands from which they had been dispossessed.

The king and his court in these days was constantly moving about from castle to castle. A crown tenant, hearing suddenly that his monarch was coming to spend the night in the lord's castle, would hastily get together food and fuel for the court's comfort. Often the king didn't pay for what he took. The lord's men sweeping through a village collecting necessities for the king were now obliged to pay the merchants.

The coming of the king to a tenant's castle or manor could mean many things. The king, of course, wanted to check on the tenant and make sure that he carried out his feudal obligations to the crown as well as to his own undertenants. Many undertenants hoped for fairer legal treatment in the courts of the king. The coming of the royal party or the periodic tours of the royal justices gave a chance to have cases heard under common law rather than local law. The decisions of the king's court had to be observed under the Charter and one of its provisions was that the sheriff (the crown deputy in the county) had to certify that the decision had been carried out.

By ancient custom, local lords dealt with their tenants in their own way, and the only law of the castle was the lord's law. Not only did this often mean, under a cruel lord, a hard life for the tenant, but it took power from the king. More and more, the Plantagenets sought to take cases from the local courts into their own courts. They did this by warning local judges that unless justice was done the case would be transferred. The barons didn't like the loss of local control and tried, unsuccessfully, to keep this power in the Charter.

As time passed, the doing of business became more important. The manors once had produced all their own food and wares. Now the towns were growing and there were more goods to be bought. Traveling peddlers passed through the land, and found no uniform standards for the amount of goods and the measures of food which they bought or sold. Chapter 35, therefore, had a provision that the weights and measures known as standard in London and the other major trading centers should be followed throughout the kingdom.

Now the Charter came to the heart of the issues between John and his lords: the just limits to royal authority. First, above all else, the subjects demanded the means of seeking justice. A freeman should not have to pay a huge fee for legal protection of his life or property. And officers of the crown must bring forth good witnesses before they charged a subject with a crime.

Most important was the assurance that the king, and later the whole government, would not prosecute by whim but by law. Whim had ruled throughout the Middle Ages, and no free society could come about until the law became strong and universal. The language of the Great Charter described the misdeeds of which John (as well as his forebears and his successors) had been guilty. Henceforth,

> *No freeman shall be taken or imprisoned or disseised or outlawed or banished, or in any way destroyed, nor will we go [march] against him, . . . except by the lawful judgment of his peers, or by the law of the land.*

To order a tenant to be captured and thrown into the dungeon of a royal castle, or to be stripped of his property or of his legal rights, or to be sent into exile was to "destroy" him as a person with rights under the feudal law. The king had no stronger punishments against a subject and they were not to be used lightly. The king was to put such penalties into effect only after a reasoned review of the charges by the subjects' peers or equals, and then only in accord with the law.

Here again, the Great Charter spoke to different ages with different meanings. The judgment of peers in the Middle Ages meant that barons could not be judged by lesser men; it was a class privilege rather than a democratic right. Nor was the judgment arrived at by the modern method of a jury trial— although for later generations, it came to require just that. The "law of the land" was one thing in the thirteenth century; it was somewhat broader in its definition in the seventeenth century when Sir Edward Coke declared it to be the inalienable right of Englishmen.

Still, the basic principle, from Chapter 39 of John's Charter to the Fifth Amendment in the Constitution of the United

States, was essentially the same: The power of government was not to be used arbitrarily to deprive anyone of the rights that were his by law. Government itself was subject to law; and an act by an officer of the government—including the king himself—was not lawful if it violated the law.

Again, the term "freemen" was to change in meaning in the next centuries. In 1215, only those holders of any rights under the tenancy system were freemen. As the feudal system broke down in the later Middle Ages, it came to mean anyone who had the right to be heard in the courts. In the modern age, all people under the government are freemen.

Chapter 39 was another shrewd example of Stephen Langton's statecraft. It wed the general opening provision of the Unknown Charter of Liberties to the particulars of a later article of the barons. Its basic importance as a constitutional proposition was almost immediately recognized. And within the same century it broke the ground for many more guarantees from later kings.

Now that the great men of the realm were safeguarded, the Charter turned to the humbler folk. Two chapters, which would later be taken from Magna Carta and expanded into a separate companion called "The Charter of the Forest," dealt with matters of daily life that affected thousands of Englishmen. Vast portions of the island were still covered with forests and many people lived by and in the woodlands.

The Normans, in taking all lands into the king's hands and then distributing certain estates to crown tenants, had made a point of keeping most forest land for the crown. The chase or hunt for deer, fox and other animals was a vital part of medieval life. Not only did it provide food to eat, but, like the tournament, it was training for the constant prospect of battle. As sport, it was royal sport, which kings from William I to John had pursued with passion. The animal life of the forest was therefore reserved for the king and such favorites as he might allow to enjoy the privileges of hunting. The dense forest was often broken abruptly by clearings. The occasional traveler might stumble upon isolated farms, or inns and wayside taverns for his comfort. In the next clearing there might nestle a small village. Apart from the deep forest were the parks and warrens where game might be hunted at the pleasure of the lord of the local estate. Here, too, tenants gathered wood for building, brush for the thatching of roofs, berries, nuts and foliage for the feeding of their swine and other farm animals.

Officers of the crown roamed these forests with a variety of special duties. The foresters and huntsmen shot and trapped the game for the king's table, and chased outlaws who killed it for themselves. Rangers drove wild boars and other dangerous beasts deep into the forest, so they would not threaten the flocks of the farms. Others, called the *vendors,* kept watch on

the greenery to see that peasants and villagers did not cut it
in forbidden areas, however much they might need it for fire-
wood, the making of brooms, or for thatching. Still a fourth
group of officers were called *agistors*. They collected the taxes
levied on farmers for the right to graze their herds of cattle or
flocks of sheep within the woodlands, and saw to it that the
animals were kept out at the seasons when newborn deer were
roaming the forests.

A separate body of forest law and custom governed the many
activities of the forests. It was administered by royal officers
in remote areas. There was no way to appeal a decree one
thought too harsh. A victim of injustice had only one recourse if
he did not want to obey—he could flee deep into the wildwood.
In this forest domain—a world of law outside the law—there
was much corruption among the king's men. A royal woodsman
might set up a tavern and force every thirsty peasant within
walking distance to patronize it. If the rangers or foresters
came upon a carcass unlawfully slain, they could charge all
dwellers in the three nearest villages with the crime, and impose
any penalty they saw fit. Men dreaded a summons to a forest
court, for here even the harsh common law was ignored.

So the tenants, in the interest of the various common people who operated and lived on their estates, sought in the
Charter to regulate the operation of the forest laws. One chapter exempted any person from having to appear before a forest
court for any general crime. Forest courts could try crimes
against forest laws alone. Another provided for the release of
lands unjustly claimed by the crown. Henry II and his sons
had dispossessed hundreds of unlucky people from lands they
had declared a part of the forest. A third chapter allowed ac-
cess to certain river banks and meadows on the countryside.
They had been forbidden to local hunters and husbandmen,
or put "in defense," so that the king might hunt undisturbed
there. The use of falcons for hunting small game was pro-

moted by this method, as the hunting party might flush quarry from the "fenced" lands. King John, who loved this sport, would take over vast tracts of land for indefinite periods. Where a crop ready for harvest was unexpectedly placed "in defense," or where small game needed for hungry peasant mouths lay in the forbidden area, the hardship was great.

Some four dozen chapters dealt with specific grievances and practices of everyday life of the great and humble. The rest of the Charter of 1215 aimed blows at John himself. He must release the English, Welsh and Scottish hostages he had seized in the course of the rebellion; he must send home his foreign troops from Poitou, and bar specific Norman and Angevin officers from positions of power in England. The tone of these chapters was that John had wrongfully imprisoned hundreds of innocent people. This was true enough, but at the same time many prisoners were held by King John simply to guarantee their good behavior or that of their relatives. King Alexander of Scotland, for one, had not joined the rebels because his two sisters were among those in John's power. The two young princesses were well treated and eventually married wealthy lords.

The concessions granted to John's opponents by the charter provisions were no guarantee, however, that their victory would be permanent. The barons had a momentary advantage, but it could slip from them almost in an instant. In the conclusion of the Great Charter they made an elaborate if clumsy attempt to keep their hold over the king. A force of twenty-five barons chosen from among the rebels was to sit in continuous judgment over John's behavior. They were to hear complaints of violations of any of the provisions of the charter. And, if the violations were not promptly corrected, they had the power to call the whole body of barons back into war against the monarch.

It was an impractical scheme—the unity of the rebels would

almost immediately fall apart, and hopes for a fair inquiry into any complaints were dim. Moreover, it went against the first premise of feudalism: the king was the paramount lord to whom all others owed fealty. For all its fine language, Magna Carta could be enforced only if the government was willing to let it be enforced. And in 1215, neither party would give in to the other, for that would put an end to all its power in the realm. One legend has it that John, when he read this conclusion, cried out, "They have given me five-and-twenty over-kings," and threw himself on the floor bellowing and chewing on straw in his helpless wrath. This story was probably wishful thinking on the part of some supporter of the barons' cause. John had little need to rage, for he had no intention of obeying any part of the Charter that infringed upon his authority. It was rather ironical, in fact, that many of the benefits that the charter stressed had been introduced by John himself. What survived in the Great Charter were those provisions that Stephen Langton had probably inserted to make all men aware of how important it was to preserve them.

These passages in the charter would appear in the reissues of the Charter during the next two years, and in the definitive reissue of 1225—ten years later—by which the fundamental importance of Magna Carta would be recognized. The charter had made certain the basic rights of freemen as the Middle Ages understood them. Beyond this, in passages like the "golden" Chapter 39, it revealed a glimpse of the rule of law that would become a reality centuries later.

Stephen Langton had served his King and his countrymen well. At the end of the long reading of the charter—which was interrupted by frequent argument and revision of chapters— the parties at length accepted it and went their way. On Friday, June 19, they met again, witnessed the great seal that was affixed to the numerous copies, and departed finally in at least nominal peace.

# 3

# The Charter
# Outlives the King

THE great seals of the realm were affixed to the copies of Stephen Langton's Great Charter on June 19, 1215. Nine weeks later, John repudiated the agreement. The pope, he said, had absolved him from honoring the grants which he had made "for us and our heirs, forever." Langton was already on his way to Rome, to defend the settlement at Runnymede, and to refute John's long catalog of accusations against him. Meantime, the barons had shown no better faith than the king —no surprise in medieval times. They sent word to Prince Louis of France that the time had come for invasion.

For the next year, the barons' and John's supporters wavered in the balance of power struggle. French forces tried to invade England and did most of the fighting. But they were unable to move the royal defenses on the Dover coast, where Hubert de Burgh skillfully defended the strongholds of the Five Ports—Dover, Hastings, Hythe, Romney and Sandwich. The two armies clashed in a definitive battle. In the fall of 1216, King John died and there was still no winner. His nine-year-old son succeeded him as the new King Henry III.

England was now in a dangerous position. With a child to be crowned, the royal party had to find some appeal that would rally the kingdom and hold the front against the rebels. Men like William Marshal, who had served with John to protect the interests of the realm, now thought of the charter of the previous year. Repudiated by John and denounced by the pope, and with its author, Stephen Langton, in virtual exile, could the document save the state in this desperate hour?

The young king's advisers took another look at the Charter. A number of them had been named in the original preamble as pledges for its performance, and with John dead the original document could prudently be edited. Twenty-two of the original sixty-three "chapters," in fact, were struck out as the council worked on a new draft. This reissue of the charter became part of the strategy for renewing the campaign against the rebels. On October 28, in the cathedral at Gloucester, the boy king was crowned and paid homage to the new papal legate, Gualo, and the Earl of Pembroke was named his guardian. Then, on November 12, under the seal of the earl, since there had been no time to cast a seal for Henry, the re-issued Magna Carta was distributed across the realm.

By this act, the crown demonstrated its good faith; the first charter had been voided, but King Henry III through his advisers was offering the same promises to his subjects and inviting them to renew their allegiance to him. The final clause in the new document was a promise to prepare still another draft of the Charter, with additional provisions desired by the subjects, once the kingdom had been restored to peace.

Thus Magna Carta of 1216, like that of 1215, was a weapon in the fight between barons and crown. Each side wanted to put the other at a psychological disadvantage. At Runnymede, the barons had wrung the Charter from the king, in defiance of feudal law, and the pope had disallowed it. A year and four months later, the king freely reissued it. It was a smart move, and was very much like the act of Henry I in taking his coronation oath. The new pope, Honorius III, endorsed the reissue. Once again he threatened to excommunicate anyone who still resisted the king; and he leveled the same threat at the French invaders who had struck without papal authority.

Almost another year passed before the civil war was finally settled. Prince Louis signed a Lenten truce in the early spring of 1217. It gave many of the rebels a chance to give up and renew their homage to Henry. The remaining barons and their French allies were routed at last at the battle of Lincoln. The French tried and failed to land a new army at the Battle of the Sandwich Islands. With the Treaty of Lambeth in September, the uprising against the Plantagenets was formally ended, and the foreign forces departed the realm.

Now the rebellion was broken and the challenge to the royalists was ended. But for the hard work and courage of one man, the crown might well have broken the promises it made to the people in the reissued charter of 1216. That man was William Marshal and he saw to it that nothing of the sort occurred. Though the rebels were not in a position to push many demands, some improvements were made in the second reissue and several new chapters were added.

The most notable change in the 1216 reissue was the separation of the single charter into two. In fact, it was only after this that the principal document came to be called *Magna Carta de Libertatibus*—the Great Charter of Liberties—to distinguish it from the more specialized *Carta de Foresta*—Charter of the Forest. Thereafter, they were both known as the Great Charters of England.

Now, in the fall of 1217, came what was in effect the final form of Magna Carta. When Henry reached his majority in 1225 and became ruler in his own right the few remaining changes would be less important than the fact that for the fourth time in a decade the charter of fundamental rights of Englishmen had been affirmed. By then, it was the only body of laws with any real value for bargaining between the crown and the lords. For generations ahead, it would be used, repeatedly, in the same way.

Since Henry III came to the throne as a young boy, his rule was a long one. In the fifty-second year of his reign, in 1267, chapter 5 of the Statute of Marlborough declared:

> The Great Charter shall be observed in all his Articles, as well as such as pertain to the King, as to the other; and that shall be enquired before the Justices in Eyre in their Circuits, and afore the Sheriffs in their Counties, when need shall be; and Writs shall be freely granted against them that do offend, before the King, or the Justices of the Bench, or before Justices in Eyre, when they come into these parts. Likewise the Charter of the Forest, shall be observed in all his Articles, and the offenders, when they be convict, shall be grievously punished by our Sovereign Lord the King . . .

It was well that the Charters were periodically restated and reenforced. Under the Plantagenet kings, peace was never certain. At times the barons were fighting for more power. At other times the king was strong enough not only to control the barons, but to send troops across the Channel to fight for the lost possessions in France. Yet somehow, in the midst of this turmoil, progress was made toward orderly government.

Henry III was not as great a ruler as the first two Henrys. He was a good enough man, but not a strong leader. He was not interested in radically changing the course of history, and he let his advisers and favorites in his court make many of his decisions for him. Nonetheless, during his long reign the realm prospered. Permanent new offices of government came into being, and the crown became less a personal government and more an institution. The Exchequer became a permanent treasury, with its own court like those of the King's Bench and Common Pleas, and Westminster began to be the permanent seat of the government.

The tenants of the mid-thirteenth century also tended to run their affairs in a more orderly way. In a pinch, armed uprisings were still the best way to settle an argument, but after the battle the barons would make sure to justify their victories by due process of law. The tenants began to demand a regular council of the realm. Here the greater lords could hear the crown's requests, and plan their response. A formal Parliament was slowly taking shape.

In 1237 the barons had granted the king's request for money after Henry agreed to reaffirm the Charters. At that time all their provisions were so well known that it was necessary only to draft a brief charter—*parva carta*—to confirm them. During the Barons' War of 1259, both parties appealed to the constitutional documents for justification. Simon de Montfort, who had married Henry's sister, had fallen out of favor with the king. Simon rallied behind him the great feudal barons to trim the powers of the crown and of the Church, for Henry III piously had rewarded the higher clergy with more power than the barons approved of.

Simon called for a grand assembly of all the kingdom's estates —including sheriffs, small freeholders and minor officials of the towns and boroughs—which met in January, 1265 as the first formal Parliament. With both Henry and his son, the Lord Edward, as virtual prisoners, de Montfort dictated his terms. These included the restraints upon the crown set out in Magna Carta and the Supplementary Provisions of Oxford of 1258. These Provisions not only urged certain rights for the barons, but, with the Provisions of Westminster added in the next year, demanded some say in how these rights were to be granted. Simon now had Henry III firmly under his thumb. Old, tired Henry was ready to put up no resistance. But Simon had not reckoned on the cleverness of young Edward. Edward saw that as Simon's power grew the barons under him were beginning to fight among themselves. He took advantage of their quarrels, and with many promises he rallied them to his cause. Simon, his forces outnumbered, was killed in battle against Edward's legions in August, 1265.

After Simon's death, the barons waited for Edward to make good on his promise for reform. Edward at last agreed and the Statute of Marlborough was issued in 1267. The constitutional power of the Charters was now guaranteed. The crown reserved the right to choose the officers of state, but taxation was a matter the king could no longer decide without consulting the Council. These compromises brought peace to the land, and young Edward could with good conscience leave old King Henry to go forth on a Crusade. On his way home, in November 1272, Henry III died, and so Edward I became the fifth Plantagenet king.

Edward was a great ruler. He inherited his father's respect for art and for beauty—Henry had seen to it that Westminster Abbey was rebuilt and consecrated in his lifetime—but he did not have Henry's love of show and extravagance. Like his grandfather, Henry II, he was a master of statesmanship. Strong in war, he was wise in peace, and made good use of the progress that had been made over the last century. The universities of Oxford and Cambridge had been founded. Henry de Bracton had written a treatise "On the Laws and Customs of England," which brought common law up to date for his time as Glanville had for the previous one. Most important, Edward saw that he could turn the demands of the crown tenants to good advantage. In return for the right to participate in Parliament the lords would take on some of the responsibility for the affairs of the realm.

The first of Edward's great statutes—enacted at the Parliament of Westminster in 1275—was in effect a detailed extension of Magna Carta. This was necessary for a more settled stage of government. The first document laid down the rules; the statutes that followed were concerned with ways to enforce the rules. The first Statute of Westminster covered many topics such as procedure in the trial of cases, the rights of women and infants, and the laws for recording documents of property rights.

Other pieces of legislation followed in rapid succession. The Statute of Gloucester in 1278 called for the barons to declare by what right they held their lands, and it ensured that each landholder would use his resources well and fairly. In 1279 the Statute of Mortmain tried to prevent gifts of land to the clergy. Once an estate was in the hands of the Church, it could never be reclaimed by the lords. The revenue from church held land went to Rome instead of to the king, which the barons found unfair and the king found expensive. Edward was the most English of English kings, and wished the church to play its proper part in the financial as well as the spiritual affairs of the nation. At this point, all he could do was to try to keep lands from falling into the dead hand, or *mortmain*, of the Church, outside of the established feudal system.

Edward took care of the merchants by enacting the 1283 Statute of Acton Burnell (which was named for the town where the Parliament met to make the law). The recording of debts was simplified, and the person who owed money could have his property taken for payment or be put in jail.

Two years later came the second Statute of Westminster, which, with the Third Statute of 1290, dealt with the inheritance and transfer of land. The laws tried to control the way land was parceled out. There were fewer great barons now, for Edward, to dilute their power, had knighted a great many lesser landholders. The result of this act, as well as from the general prosperity of the nation, was the creation of a great middle class. The king, by feudal custom, had granted land to the lords; these overlords in turn parceled it out to various tenants; now the tenants themselves were passing on the land by leasing it to members of this growing middle class. The new subtenants were paying their feudal obligations to the tenants, and the barons were jealous. They wished these new subtenants to serve them directly. But the new laws did not serve just the interests of the overlord. Since the new tenants in effect could now pass on both land and its obligations to new landholders the way was now open for land to be treated as property, something one could buy or sell.

In fact, much of the old feudal pattern was now changing. Knight service itself was all but a thing of the past. Tenants, instead of arming themselves to fight their overlord's battles, could pay their shield money, so the lord could hire his own professional soldiers. And Edward had, in the Statute of Winchester, begun the organization of a police force for each city and district, and had local officers chosen to keep the peace in each area.

Edward I had accounted for more basic legislation in the first fifteen years of his reign than any ruler since the Roman Emperor Justinian. He was a most forward-looking king, studying the way other countries ran their affairs, and meeting the leaders of the kingdoms of Europe. He knew that feudalism would have to change to keep pace with the times.

If Edward had any serious fault, it was in moving ahead as fast as he did. The landed barons were worried that with his growing popularity, the king might become ever more powerful. They had been able to browbeat Henry III, but not Edward.

The king's program of legislation had continually moved toward a more democratic government for all of England. But for years after the Parliament of 1295, the barons pressed the king to give in to more constitutional limitations on the crown. In the end, even though he met his tenants' demands, the king added to the accomplishments of his own legislation; for in confirming the Great Charters during 1297, he also for the first time made them a formal part of the statutes of the realm.

Pressed by the barons for a statement that he would abide by the Charters, Edward responded with two documents. The first, later called the Charter of Inspeximus, opened with the statement, "We have examined the Great Charters of Henry our father," and, after reciting their passages in detail, concluded that "we herewith ratify the same." Edward then followed Inspeximus with a Confirmation of the Charters, which left no doubt of his willingness and intention to make them the supreme law of the land.

The "Charter of Liberties, and the Charter of the Forest, which were made by Common Assent of all the Realm, in the time of King Henry our Father, shall be kept in every point without breach," Edward declared. To prove his good faith, he directed that copies of both charters should be sent to all officers of the realm and "published" by being read aloud in the town market places and the churches, and further, that all courts of the realm "shall allow the said Charters pleaded before them in all their Points."

Edward thus warned the courts to allow "actions on the charters," that is, claims could be made on the specific guarantees of the charters themselves rather than on formal writs of common law. Magna Carta was now planted in the very heart of the law itself. It was, in many ways, the crowning accomplishment of Edward's great program of private law. Constitutional principles were set side by side with private rights of individual freemen. Throughout the medieval period, constitutional government had a stunted growth at best. The Great Charter might never have survived to modern times had not Edward added it into the body of statutes, so that any of its provisions could be pleaded in actions at law.

Edward's Confirmation of the Charters was clear. It set aside any court proceedings "against the points of the Charters," provided that both documents should be read aloud to the congregations in the cathedrals of the land twice a year, and directed that bishops should excommunicate "all those that by Word, Deed, Aid or Counsel do contrary." The Confirmation then went on to add other assurances, that emergency "aids, tasks and prises" should not be "drawn into a Custom"—that is, made a regular form of royal income thereafter.

For another century, Plantagenets would cling to the hope that they could recapture the old empire. And so England naturally took part in wars of succession on the Continent. This led to extraordinary demands upon the resources of the tenants. "Aids" had now come to mean goods and cattle requisitioned for the mainland adventures; "tasks" were special taxes for war purposes; and *prises* were "takings" of any sort that the crown deemed necessary for the emergency. In general, the lords supported the king without complaint. But they demanded written declarations that the levies would end when the emergency passed. Edward went further, and agreed that thereafter the special levies would be approved by Parliament. In its concluding chapter, the Confirmation agreed to remove a special tax on wool imports; this showed how important the non-military tenants were, and the new large role played by trade in the life of the country.

The Confirmations were first signed by the king's son in London on October 10, then taken across the Channel to the camp of the king himself, where the great seals were affixed on November 25, 1297.

Edward I made one further change in Magna Carta. Since the very beginning of the Charters in 1215, the barons had been trying to find a way to enforce them. But "there was no punishment established for them which offended against the points of the Charters." In 1300, accordingly, the king agreed to a list of twenty Articles on the Charters. These articles were like amendments to a constitution. They dealt with specific abuses both of Magna Carta and of Carta de Foresta that were thereafter to be specifically punished in the royal courts.

Known as *Articuli super Cartas,* or articles beyond the Charters, the document was significant in another respect. It was drafted by Parliament itself. Parliament had begun to make the laws. Earlier, Parliament had only commented on laws initiated by the crown. This move by Parliament was a forerunner of those times in the fourteenth and early fifteenth centuries when the confirmation of the Great Charters would originate in Parliament, not in the crown. In fact, this circumstance caused Edward I to complain to the Pope that the Articles of 1300 had been forced upon him in contradiction of feudal theory. The law had always in the past gone from the crown to his council and then, in final form, back to the crown for a general proclamation to the public.

The See of Rome did not respond with the speed of Innocent III after Runnymede, mainly because the involvements of European politics complicated the question, and because the idea of a joint participation in the rule of the kingdom was not as revolutionary as it had been eighty-five years before. In any event, Edward I died in 1307 without the Pope's repudiation of the Articles, and they settled into the body of law with the Charters themselves. Indeed, in another companion statute, *de Tallagio non Concedendo,* Parliament also stated that "tallages" (taxes for the crown's use as it saw fit) were not to be approved. Thus the English revolutionists of the seventeenth century could turn to a key argument against fund-raising by the King without authorization by Parliament.

The details in the Articles showed the further growth and complexity of feudal life as the fourteenth century began. Eleven of the twenty chapters dealt with the proper division of the work of government between the courts and other agencies of the crown. Three limited the functions of the sheriff, three others tried to regulate the behavior of juries and lawyers, and the final chapter, describing "standards for working gold and silver," was another sign of the growth of the economy.

The royal court still roved from place to place in England, and so the old questions of purveyances continued to vex the authorities. Chapter 2 of the Articles therefore tried to spell out in greater detail the responsibilities of all parties in these transactions. It was not until the government joined the royal courts in a permanent seat at Westminster, however, that the problem could be resolved. The activities of some new officers of the crown, whose offices and duties had been created to meet the needs of changing times, also caused problems. The coroner, a general investigator of matters affecting the crown succeeded the sheriff as the chief royal officer in many counties—and upset the order of business whenever he passed through the vicinity. The King's marshal was a special officer who prosecuted crimes within the *verge*—a twelve-mile radius around the traveling court wherever it went.

The crown's judicial officers tended to push for greater and greater power. It was part of the growth toward a truly national government. It had begun under Henry I with the first circuit judges, who had gradually taken over the main body of criminal law from local courts. The growth of the system of writs followed, and the great assizes whereby a tenant could argue his claim of dispossession in the king's courts or under king's law rather than in the courts of his local lord.

Regular royal courts developed—King's Bench (crimes and other state actions), Common Pleas (civil suits between subjects) and Exchequer (tax and related matters)—and with them, a running fight between them over where their respective responsibilities began and ended. The furthest away from the king's control were the local courts dating from Saxon times— courts of the shire or county and of the hundred (an area with a population of a hundred families) which took care of affairs of local government as well as dealing with petty complaints. In between, waging a losing fight for survival, were the manorial or seigneurial courts of the lords of the various estates, which once had dealt with all questions arising from the holding or

working of land, and any other disputes affecting their own subtenants or villeins.

There were also the forest courts, whose special problems
and abuses prompted the advisers of Henry III to draft a separate charter dealing with them; on the coast at the seaport
towns were admiralty courts, concerned with the maritime laws
of trade over the seas; at the trade fairs were less formal courts
to determine the laws of trade common to England and Europe.
The courts at the fairs, where travelers often appeared with
the dust of the highways still on their feet, won the picturesque

name of "courts of pie powder," from the *pie poudre* or dusty feet of the complaining parties.

A large body of important law was also administered by the ecclesiastical courts; canon law covered not only the behavior of the churchmen and their followers and servants, but also matters of wills and the distribution of property of those who died without wills (intestates). Marriages and the legitimacy of heirs were also the special province of the spiritual courts or "courts Christian." The Jews had their own Exchequer for settling commercial matters between themselves, although other judicial matters involving them were the concern of the king himself.

This vast network of overlapping courts, which had developed by the end of the thirteenth century, needed a specially-trained body of lawyers to cope with legal questions. The first "law schools"—groups of men studying the law together in inns near the courts at Westminster—dated from the latter part of the reign of Henry III. Sometimes, both the King and Parliament had to interfere to straighten matters out. And so a great deal of attention was given to the subject of courts and their officers in the Articles on the Charters.

Aside from the glimpse of the judicial structure in England at this time, the final chapter in the Articles was the most revealing of all. It decreed that no gold- or silversmith could thereafter use anything but gold of a certain "touch" or "silver of the sterling alloy." The finished articles would then be stamped with a hallmark to certify that the craftsmen supervising the work in the particular guild hall had examined it and given a stamp of approval. The "touch of Paris" was decreed the standard of fineness for gold, while sterling silver was a standard taken from certain guilds of craftsmen in Germany.

The chapter spoke much about the metal crafts and also the economic habits of the realm at this time. Men trained from childhood in the use of "touchstones" could develop a keen eye for the distinguishing mark that these stones—usually quartz or jasper—left on metal of a certain refinement. The guildsmen of Paris had developed a "touch" for gold that became in the Middle Ages the mark of gold's quality, just as "karat" denotes its quality today. Masters whose eyes had been trained to recognize a mark produced by this "touch" were alone licensed to approve the work of their guilds and to stamp it with a distinguishing leopard's head.

Insurance against impurities in metal was needed in this age when coins were regularly clipped and remelted. A prosperous lord might change his gold and silver into plate and ornamental pieces. With a hallmark stamped upon it, this would be as good as or better than the coin of the realm. It was important, therefore, to make sure that craftsmen did not substitute base metals in the manufacturing process.

The medieval world was changing. The appearance of Parliament, the expansion of courts, the founding of the universities and the "inns of court," the numbers of great constitutional statutes to deal with new interests and activities, the rise of the wool export trade and the supervision of the craft guilds— all these concerns gave a clue to the new directions the next century would take.

For the older feudal system would begin to break down when lords of the fee could no longer depend completely upon the land. It was still too early for a significant trade economy, but when the old system of tenancies died out a new economy would become inevitable.

In the fourteenth and fifteenth centuries the philosophies and governmental processes of the Middle Ages would begin to break down as well. For another hundred years the remarkable house of the Angevins would continue to rule, and flashes of the old Norman glory would be glimpsed in the early military successes of Edward III. Another moment of triumph for the old empire would be realized under Henry V of Lancaster, but his premature death and the bloody rivalry of the royal houses of Lancaster and York would lead to the long Wars of the Roses with which the Middle Ages would expire.

The thread linking these trends and events was the play for power between the monarchy and the great lords. Their means to this power would be the strengths and weaknesses of Parliament and its laws, straining to adapt to a tumultuous age.

# 4

# The Charter
# Outlives the Age

THE chronic political problem of the Middle Ages was how to keep the crown from despotism without opening the way for greater despotism from the barons. No answer was found throughout the fourteenth and fifteenth centuries, nor until the English Revolution in the seventeenth century. Plantagenet fortunes steadily declined after the death of Edward I except for the first years of the reign of Edward III. Yet Edward III's very achievements on the battlefield began the ruinous campaigns of the Hundred Years' War between England and France.

In this troubled century the Angevin dynasty came to an end with the fall of the inglorious Richard II. In the years after his death the country was torn by the sporadic Wars of the Roses as the Houses of Lancaster and York fought for control of the English throne.

> *So shaken as we are, so wan with care,*
> *Find we a time for frightened peace to pant,*

pleaded Shakespeare's Henry IV at the midway point in these dread two centuries.

In these violent years, survival was uncertain for men and ideas alike. Parliament asserted its will when it could, but Parliament could meet only at the pleasure of the king, and the only way it could pressure the crown was by demanding a *quid pro quo*—giving up one thing to get another. The king usually had to reaffirm the Great Charters in return for the right to tax. The royal confirmations tended to become a routine without much meaning, but they nonetheless served as reminders from generation to generation that there was such a thing as a fundamental law that ought to control men's actions.

Edward II, like many sons who follow dominating fathers, paled by comparison with the great constitution-builder, nor was he very keen for military adventure. Strong men among the lords, measuring his mettle, decided that they could use him for their own purposes. But the second Edward, while he was not forceful, was not one to be cowed either. The reign became a seesaw of rivalries, as the Earl of Lancaster, ambitious and unscrupulous, began a series of intrigues that would lead his successors, generations later, to the throne.

Since John's reign, the barons had organized a directorate which, like the committee of twenty-five proposed in the first draft of Magna Carta, was designed to make the king their puppet. In the last years of Henry III, they had called themselves the Lords Conservators, protectors of the realm. In an effort to bring Edward II under their control, another group of barons called themselves the Lords Ordainers, for the list of "ordinances" or special decrees that they drafted. In the last years of Richard II, they were the Lords Appellant, lodging "appeals" (criminal charges) against their rivals and political foes.

Edward II, like Stephen two centuries before, meant well but accomplished little. He rallied an army to put down a Scottish uprising in 1314, but the result was a disaster. The king led a huge army to face the Scottish hero, Robert the Bruce, at Bannockburn. The Scots, although outnumbered almost three to one, slaughtered thousands of Englishmen and broke Edward's power over Scotland. Until the House of Stuart linked the thrones a hundred years later, Scotland remained an independent government. During the black years that followed the break with Scotland, England was in chaos. Edward had so little control over the barons that the Earl of Lancaster set up his own court and even called his own parliaments within Edward's realm.

At last, in 1322, King Edward was able to defeat Lancaster and have him executed as a traitor; but peace lasted only a few years. Edward's Queen, Isabella of France, deserted him and returned to Paris. Edward was foolish enough to let her son, the crown prince, follow her. The fierce and wily Roger Mortimer, one of the mightiest lords with holdings on the marches, or borderlands, of Wales, had joined her in Paris. He intended to have both England and the Queen, and by the winter of 1327, he had succeeded. He and Isabella rallied Edward II's enemies around the young prince and, with a large army behind them, sailed for England. The king's forces were routed. Edward himself was captured and made to give up his crown. He was taken to Berkeley Castle, where he was murdered. It was whispered that his queen's lover ordered him tortured to death with hot pokers.

Mortimer, now the Earl of March, ruled the land through the Queen Mother Isabella and the youthful Edward III, but his hold on power slipped after less than three years. For the next three decades, the House of Anjou would rise to its final brilliance. The third of the Edwards, although scarcely more than a boy, took the reins of government firmly in hand. He threw off his advisers, and at eighteen he ordered Mortimer executed for the murder of his father. He quelled the Scottish barons in 1333 and, a dozen years later, scattered the French armies in a series of dazzling victories climaxed by the Battle of Crècy.

In the midst of Edward's reign, and in the midst of the century, the bubonic plague, the Black Death, moved like divine retribution across the face of warring Europe. For three years and more it ravaged all the nations, claiming two million lives in England alone. And as it passed over the lands, it crumbled the foundations of the feudal system. Scores of villages lay abandoned. Livestock was slaughtered for lack of men to tend them. Farmland lay fallow. When the disease had run its course, the lords of estates could not restore the old system. There were few enough laborers and so much work that the lords had to plead or bargain or fight for the tenants paravail to work the land once again. The lords found that they could rent the farms to independent yeomen at greater profit. Many poor farm workers claimed abandoned land for cattle instead of crops. Hundreds of men whose fathers and grandfathers had been bound to the soil now began to move to the towns to work at clothmaking. By the last half of the fourteenth century, England's future as a manufacturing and exporting nation was beginning to take shape.

The ten years following the Black Death saw Edward's reign move toward its climax. After another brilliant victory over the French at Poitiers, a treaty of settlement brought the great province of Aquitaine back under English rule. It had been a century and a half since King John had lost the old Norman empire. However, France had the greater resources in manpower and goods, and the balance of power would shift again. Although there would still be the brief glory of Henry V's recapture of Normandy, the Hundred Years' War would end with the permanent retirement of England from the Continent.

Edward III had the misfortune to outlive his own glory. In his last years he saw the hard-won French possessions torn from him, and his treasury bankrupted by war. He saw the plague, which wiped out a third of his subjects, kill his own wife, Queen Phillipa.

His heir apparent had been his son, the dashing Black Prince of Crècy and Poitiers; but the prince's administration of

Aquitaine was a disaster and he died before his father. An ambitious new leader, John of Gaunt, married the heiress of the earldom of Lancaster; he prepared the way for the final triumph of the Lancasters over the Plantagenets. Edward's powers failed. He consoled himself with the riches of his court, and with his mistresses, and slipped quietly into senility. In 1377, Edward died, dishonored and alone, and the throne descended to his ten-year-old grandson, Richard of Bordeaux, the son of the Black Prince.

During Edward's last years the shape of English government had changed. The House of Commons long had been reduced to assembling dutifully in one chamber at Westminster until their superiors told them what legislative actions had been taken. Now they demanded a voice in the deliberations. Nearly eighty years had passed since the "great and model Parliament" of 1295 had brought together all estates of the realm, both great and small. Yet even then, as in the Parliaments under Edward II and Edward III, the Commons had been allowed to do no more than listen to decisions already made.

In the past the mystical superiority of the overlords had kept the Commons meek. They had obediently voted taxes to finance the constant warfare. The Commons did not think of threatening to withhold taxes as a price for a voice in legislation. But now the day was at hand when the Commons would press for advantage.

Taxes, always a painful issue, had risen with the cost of the war with France and had produced a revolution in young King Richard's reign. Three years after he was crowned, the short and terrible Peasants' War broke out. It was a sign of the final end of feudalism; the rebels lashed out against the centers of baronial power and against the religious houses with their own vast estates. Slaughtering the agents of their overlords, they stole the charters and other documents of their serfdom and destroyed them. What the Black Death had begun, the Peasants' War completed. It was hardly more than an angry crowd that got out of hand, and when order was restored its leaders were all promptly executed. But the significance of the Peasants' War lay not in its size but in its message. Now feudalism was practically, as well as economically, dead.

Richard's handling of the issues in the uprising set the course of his inglorious reign. He granted all of the peasant leaders' demands when he met them on the outskirts of London —though he had no intention of keeping any of his promises. He and his lords were thunderstruck by the boldness of the revolt, which overthrew the whole feudal system of obligations. What a shock it must have been to see the values held by generations of ancestors overturned in a summer.

The next few years brought only greater troubles. Richard's first marriage produced no heirs and he married a French princess to seal a peace treaty with her father. Since she was only seven years old, he had to face the fact that in all likelihood the House of Anjou would die with him. Abroad, the war with France continued to go against England, while the Scots again were raiding along the borders. His uncles, the dukes of Lancaster and Gloucester, dominated him. He briefly broke away from their control, but they denounced his new advisers, organized the Lords Appellants, and executed all who had supported Richard.

The young king in due course struck back. He had Gloucester murdered and exiled his cousin, Henry of Bolingbroke. When Henry's father, John of Gaunt, died, Richard declared the inheritance forfeit. Yet Richard was caught in the web of his own plotting. His chief justice was drawn and quartered by the king's enemies. People began to say the king was going mad, and they were probably right. Government had come practically to a standstill as Richard took up an old custom and roamed aimlessly over the land with his court.

The end came swiftly. In the summer of 1399, Henry of

Bolingbroke landed on the northeastern coast of England and men came to his support from all over the land. Richard returned from Ireland with most of the royalist forces and ran headlong into an ambush. Within six months, he died in a castle prison, probably murdered on Bolingbroke's orders. After two and a half centuries, the reign of the Angevins had ended as ingloriously as the reign of the Normans.

Throughout his rule, Henry of Bolingbroke was obsessed with the accusation that he had seized the throne. After all, if Richard, childless, had died a natural death Henry might have been offered the crown anyway. And the murderous jealousies between the great houses of the realm—a century of war between Lancaster and York was yet to come—made it doubtful whether any succession to the throne could have been accomplished bloodlessly. Yet Henry strove to prove he was the king indeed by behaving as a just king should. After falling into ruin under Richard, the government needed to be put in good order, and to this Henry applied himself. He showed his good faith by repeatedly confirming the Great Charters before Parliament.

Neither the men of his time nor the historians who would later judge him gave him much credit. The Scots grew restless; but Richard held the northern border by keeping hostages in the Tower of London. The Welsh rose up in a vigorous war of independence; but under the generalship of Henry's son and heir to the crown, the threat was beaten down. The House of Percy twice rose in rebellion and twice was defeated. But when the kingdom at last settled into relative quiet, Henry himself had become a sick and weary old man. Shakespeare caught the tragedy of his life in his deathbed words to his son:

> *God knows, my son,*
> *By what by-paths and indirect crook'd ways*

*I met this crown; and I myself know well*
*How troublesome it sat upon my head . . .*
       *. . . It seem'd in me*
*But as an honor snatch'd with boisterous hand;*
*And I had many living to upbraid*
*My gain of it by their assistances; . . .*
*For all my reign hath been but as a scene*
*Acting that argument . . .*

Bolingbroke's son was crowned Henry V when he was only twenty-six. He had proved himself a valiant fighter. He also was trained in the arts of government, for he had helped in many of the royal duties in his father's' helpless last days. A new age of glory seemed to be dawning. The dashing and vigorous monarch who now had all of England, Scotland and Wales kneeling before him could look abroad with daring plans for an empire vaster than that of the early Angevins. France was torn by civil wars and the old Norman duchy lay temptingly open to recapture. But young Henry was thinking even more grandly. His ultimate goal was a permanent union of the crowns of France and England.

Henry soon found an excuse for invasion. He won a series of battles in Normandy and deathless fame in history and literature for his stunning victory at Agincourt. The houses of Orleans and Burgundy were now fighting each other. Henry set out to back the likely winner so as to insure his own claims in France. The mad King of France, Charles VI, had an eligible daughter, the Princess Catherine. Since the French throne could be handed down through the princess, the English king's great dream seemed now within reach.

A treaty was soon drawn up between the kingdoms. England once more ruled the ancient Angevin empire. Henry and Catherine were to marry; and, in addition, if young Henry outlived Charles, he would have the French crown as well. How practical this arrangement might have been we will never know. By a quirk of fate the strong and triumphant Henry suddenly fell ill and died. He left his young French Queen alone in a strange land with an infant son. A council of regents would have to rule for the prince for years to come. Suddenly the government was drifting on an ebbing tide. The dream of great empire quickly faded. A foreign empire was an expensive glory, and now that the great ruler was gone the people complained more loudly about the heavy taxation. The regency soon learned how hard it was to rule from both London and Paris. To make matters worse, many were tempted, during the heir's long minority, to overthrow the Lancastrians altogether. While the uncle of young Henry VI was away reviving the English government in the Continental provinces, enemies of the Lancastrians worked against him at home. Abroad he had to cope with a French offensive under the crusading Joan of Arc.

Henry VI, in fact, was doomed to a reign in which almost everything failed. By the middle of the century, all his father's European gains had been lost. Parliament again had almost ceased to function. And although Henry had married Margaret of Anjou, for many years they had no children. At last a son was born, but many doubted that he was legitimate.

The trusting, scholarly Henry VI was not equipped to deal with the difficulties of his times. For a period he lost his mind, and York was named "Protector" of the king, which was something like putting a hungry wolf in charge of a fat sheep. A dynastic struggle between the dukes of York and Somerset flared into the Wars of the Roses in 1454. After Somerset died in battle six months later, York's power grew stronger. Intermittently, trouble broke out. Partisans of one side or the other would attack local areas. At best there was a tense peace; often parts of the country were in turmoil. Henry tried to launch an attack upon his "protector" but he was quickly captured and persuaded to name the duke as the successor to the throne. Thus, by his own act, he cast further doubt on the legitimacy of his own son.

York himself was killed in battle a few months later, but his son Edward came to London, proclaimed himself king, and by winning the Battle of Towton forced Henry to flee to Scotland. For the next ten years, there were nominally two kings of England, but Henry's hope of returning to power was gone. Henry's wife, Queen Margaret, urged the Lancastrians to join the Scots and the French in several invasions. The attacks were unsuccessful, and at the battle of Tewkesbury in 1471, the queen was captured, her son, the young prince, was slain, and Henry was led back to the Tower of London to be murdered. With the House of Lancaster now destroyed, Edward IV was secure on the throne. The last years of his reign were peaceful, and the king turned from warfare to the luxuries of his wealth and his court. He died unexpectedly of illness in 1483, when he was only 41 years old.

Edward V was the late king's son, but he was never crowned. A boy of 12 when his father died, he and his younger brother Richard were placed in the Tower of London by their uncle, the Duke of Gloucester, for their "safety." The Duke then claimed that both of the boys had been born through witchcraft. He, the only true son of the Duke of York still living, was the only legitimate successor to the throne. While citizens of the realm remained confused by this claim, Gloucester struck swiftly in early June. Within a matter of weeks he had arrested and killed the strongest supporters of the Queen Mother. By July 6—less than a hundred days after the death of Edward IV—the "reign" of Edward V was over and Richard III was crowned. His body small and deformed, one shoulder hitched higher than the other, he made up in craft and genius for what he lacked in charm. For much of his life he had been, at least on the surface, a loyal subject, but now he revealed himself as a clever and dangerous man. He made sure to secure his claim to the throne by murdering the two young princes in the Tower.

Richard's own bloody reign was short. As if he were aware that he had little time, he summoned Parliament back into session and made a show of proposing a number of legislative reforms. His reforms never took effect in his short lifetime, and the King didn't seem to take much interest in them. But the session was nonetheless very important. During the years of civil war both Parliament and the king had ignored many workaday problems in the realm. For a century the lesser gentry who made up the House of Commons had been more interested in a new age of business and trade than in good government, while the great lords fought their own bloody battles. This Parliament showed that both the king and the people were aware the new age required some action by the government. Commercial banking was in its primitive beginnings. Trade was taking up more of the energies of a new middle class. And land was being transferred to new holders, releasing both the old and the new holders from their feudal obligations.

Richard's Parliament of 1484 was the first to meet in more than twenty years. Richard promised that another would convene soon thereafter, and we can assume he meant to keep his word. But the people of England were no longer so ready to support him. In less than a decade, Christopher Columbus would discover a new world and the narrow horizons of medievalism would vanish forever. Richard's way of murdering his rivals amounted to a reign of terror, and England's citizens longed for someone who could bring an end to the long years of misery.

The end came on August 21, 1485, near the town of Bosworth in the central part of England. Henry of Richmond, with an army of exiles who had fled from Richard's cruelty, met the king in a pitched battle. Although his cause was lost,

Richard did not flee the field. He died bravely, and his crown, which he had worn all through the fighting, was placed then and there on the head of Henry Tudor. The dark ages had finally run their course, and the age of the House of Tudor was now to begin. "England hath long been mad, and scarr'd herself," said Shakespeare's Earl of Richmond. The new Henry VII, and the whole land, prayed:

> *Enrich the time to come with smooth-fac'd peace,*
> *With smiling plenty, and with prosperous days.*

In the long century of Lancastrian and Yorkist rule and rivalry, Parliament had met no more than a dozen times. During the reign of the Tudor kings, Parliament came into more importance. Under Henry VII it met six times, and under Henry VIII sixteen. What was more important, many more laws were enacted under the Tudors, who saw the needs of a nation that was developing a large trade over the seas. While a struggle with the Roman Church was the most spectacular element in the statecraft of Henry VIII, it overshadowed the more important economic advances that he brought about at the same time.

When Henry VII came into control of the English throne, he was busy foiling plots to overthrow him and with fighting France. But the Tudors were realistic. They were more interested in the middle-class activities of the new age than in trying to recover the past glory of feudalism. By the time the sixteenth century opened, the kingdom was settling into peace and Parliament was making laws on modern issues of personal and property rights that could be settled in court. Henry VII was a calm ruler who assumed that if he worked for a better life for his subjects, they would work for him. Where the medieval kings had used pomp and ritual to gain vows of obedience and military backing, Henry VII managed his own

government like a modern businessman. He spoke the same language as the new merchant adventurers of the realm.

Thus, after two hundred years of chaotic government, a better new world came into being. It was an age of discovery that was not only geographic but intellectual. The Renaissance in arts and literature and the Reformation in religion were spreading their liberal ideas through all of Western Europe.

The English Church demanded independence, and would have asked for it even if Henry VIII had not challenged Rome with his plea for a "divorce."

Perhaps the most important event of all in bringing about the modern age in England was the introduction of printing. A hunger for information was both stimulated and made possible by printing presses, which told of England's past history and of new ideas abroad in the world. Among the many books that spread new ideas were major works on the law. One work by an English judge named Thomas Littleton, *On Tenures,* summarized the ancient feudal rights and liabilities of landholding. Completed near the end of the Yorkist period, it would later be elaborately edited by Sir Edward Coke in the early seventeenth century. Under the general title of *Coke on Littleton,* it was to preserve until modern times the medieval language used in dealing with property.

Another fifteenth-century work was *De Laudibus Legum Anglie,* by Sir John Fortescue. He stressed the advantages of the common law system in the development of the English constitution. Supposedly written for the education of Henry VI's son, Edward, it became instead a summary of the surviving principles of law even in the chaos of the evil times. There was a difference between the idea of law in absolute monarchies and in the English ideal of limited monarchies. In absolute monarchies, "whatever pleased the king had the force of law," if the king said so. But in England "the king rules his people not only regally but also politically, and so he is bound by oath at his coronation to the observance of his law."

That these ideas were written down even in a time of turmoil in the land showed that the principles of the Great Charters were still alive. Now that there was printing many could read Fortescue's work after its appearance in 1545. Littleton's work was printed as early as 1528, under the editorship of John Rastell. Rastell was a legal historian whose popular history, *A Pastime of People,* appeared the following year. One of the historical episodes in this history that excited Englishmen of the age was the story of Runnymede. Wide numbers of people were learning the lessons of Magna Carta. The Wars of the Roses had cut down many of the old nobility. The rise of the House of Commons under Henry VIII and his daughter, Elizabeth I, would all but complete the process. Henry was able to push through Parliament his laws for the independence of the Church of England by getting the support of the lesser gentry in Commons, as well as that of the lords. Commons thus became aware of its own power, and worked to assert it under Henry's successors, Mary I and Elizabeth I. These attempts were not really very successful. But during the long and peaceful reign of Elizabeth— "Good Queen Bess"—Commons was laying the groundwork for its power in the next century.

Commons, in fact, already provided the voice for a steadily growing class of freemen—country squires, merchants and lawyers. Vast tracts of Church lands were seized during the Reformation when the Church of England broke with the Roman Church. And the government paid for many of its needs by selling these lands to the gentry. While some of the feudal language still clung to these transfers of land title, no one paid much attention to the old ideas of obligations and services that went with the land. And so a new middle class was created that had no roots in medievalism. As this middle class came to dominate the House of Commons, the English monarchy would hear louder and louder demands for a more democratic sort of government.

The Tudor century thus brought England from the Middle Ages into modern times. Numerous royal courts sprang up to administer the lands and laws once claimed as the right of the Church, but the common law courts steadily undercut their authority and in time triumphed over them. Most of the administration of local justice was turned over to justices of the peace, a position of honor that was in striking contrast to the old courts of the shire and the hundred.

By the time of Elizabeth's death in 1603, modern England was already recognizable. England had become a major maritime power by defeating the Spanish Armada and was soon to plant its first permanent colony in the New World. It had a government with one of the first legislative bodies that could work separately from a sovereign. It was also a nation of skilled artisans and gifted artists—and learned thinkers in the law.

The last years of Elizabeth's reign had marked the rise of the brilliant attorney whose ideas would reshape the whole concept of English common law. He would make clear for his time the meaning of the Great Charter of Liberties and cement it as the cornerstone of the English constitution. Sir Edward Coke (usually pronounced *Cook*) served the Queen as her Attorney-General, the chief legal officer of the government. Just before her death she made him Chief Justice of the Court of Common Pleas. In this position he prepared the *Reports* on decided cases. His reports and findings were the starting point for modern court practices.

For Coke, the rule of law without personal influences and tested by the experience of the centuries, was the key to a free society. "The King is under no man, but under God and the law," he once said to James I. And though he was reported to have then begged his King's forgiveness, he did not take back his words. He consistently claimed that government itself was subject to the law. And he cited Magna Carta as his authority, causing James to dismiss him from the bench in 1616.

This gave the increasingly aggressive House of Commons its greatest champion, for Coke was elected to the House almost immediately after his dismissal. It would be here, and in his monumental *Institutes* on English law—including a full volume on the Great Charter—that he would lay the foundation stones for the modern English constitution, a towering achievement that won him lasting fame.

# 5

# Cornerstone of the English Constitution

IT is often said that the English constitution is unwritten. And in the sense that it is not a single document, this is true. But it *is* written—in the words of four fundamental documents from the Parliamentary struggles of the seventeenth century. With these documents the claim of the "divine right" of kings ended forever.

The Tudors had been clever enough to keep the restless Parliament in check, but the Stuarts were neither so lucky nor so skilled. At first, it had appeared that the new king would be able to maintain the balance between throne and Commons. James had been crowned as a baby in Scotland and had ruled that rugged land for forty years. He was used to the constant plotting between Presbyterians pushing their new beliefs and Roman Catholics trying to hold to the old ways. That had become a political struggle as well as a religious one. The king of the Scots had had to play off the various interests against each other.

Since the triumphant days of the great David Bruce and his father Robert, who had won Scotland for the Scots when the hapless Edward II was king of England, efforts had been made to unite the two crowns. Throughout the Middle Ages, whenever England faced a war on the Continent, she risked the Scots striking from the north. For whenever the hardy Highlanders were not attacking on their own, they were in league with France. The English cut down the danger by taking Scottish hostages whenever they could. But there was always a hope that the troubles would end and the two kingdoms would be united under a single crown. After all, they shared a common language and common traditions, and many of their interests and needs were similar.

With the Scottish King James VI, the hope seemed about to be realized, even though his mother—the famous Mary, Queen of Scots—was first a hostage, then a prisoner and finally a victim of English Church politics. In 1586 James and Queen Elizabeth made an alliance that made him the probable successor to the English throne. After agreeing to this arrangement, Elizabeth felt that she could safely execute Mary without fear of a general Scottish uprising. She was right. Although there were strong protests north of the border, James clung to the promises in his year-old treaty with Elizabeth and let the beheading pass, without taking any military or political action against the Queen.

James had never known his mother, for she had left him a baby in Scotland when she herself lost the desperate game of power politics between the Reformation and Catholic parties. Mary was a granddaughter of Henry VII. She and Elizabeth were cousins, and at one time they talked of the chance of the survivor gaining the other's throne. Mary was driven from her throne by the outraged Scots for plotting with her lover to murder her husband, James' father. She then fled to England seeking Elizabeth's protection. Eventually, Elizabeth decided that the executioner's axe was the only way to keep Mary from trying for the English throne.

This bloody family life left James a worldly-wise ruler but a stern personality. When he finally united the Scottish and

English crowns, he had two unshakable convictions upon which to base a policy of government. One was that a king was chosen of God, and while the monarch might listen to the advice of counselors or parliaments, the king's will must prevail. The other conviction was that Protestant Reformers were troublemakers, whether in the pulpit or in Parliament. That fiery seeker of justice, John Knox, had given him much trouble in Scotland.

Thus a single-minded king, lacking the charm and flexibility of the great queen he succeeded, came up short against a stubborn parliament. It spelled unhappiness for himself, and disaster for his son, Charles I. James was able to avoid a final showdown with the House of Commons, although he personally tore a page from the journals of the Commons which was a famous Protestation asserting that "the liberties, franchises, privileges and jurisdictions of Parliament are the ancient and undoubted birthright and inheritance of the subjects of England."

Sir Edward Coke had written that Protestation. He was also to be the spiritual father of the Petition of Right which, seven years later, would become the cornerstone of the English constitution. As a "Parliament man," Coke had suggested that the Chapter of Magna Carta protecting the rights of all free men* contained the seed of the Constitution that was still in force in Coke's day. Bills in the House of Commons aimed at curbing the crown's claims of divine right were called "Magna Carta bills." These bills had succeeded in getting through the Protestation describing Commons' right to make laws prohibiting imprisonment by the crown without good cause.

When James became king, Commons determined to use its power over money matters to bully the king, if necessary. In medieval times and under the strong-willed Tudors, Commons

* Chapter 29, numbered 39 in the original charter of 1215.

had never dared to try this strong action, and a man like James did not take the move kindly. Unable to get the funds he wanted from Parliament, the king cast about for authority to raise money under a royal right. Magna Carta, he told himself, could work both ways. There was a power granted the king, or the paramount lord, to demand a "benevolence" or free-will grant of money from his subjects. Used in feudal times, this chapter of the Magna Carta had not recently been appealed to, but no one had repealed it. The Plantagenets had even developed the Privy Seal (a private seal for the king's personal affairs) with this feudal right in mind. Documents bearing the stamp of the Privy Seal could enforce the personal services due the sovereign just as if they were official state decrees bearing the Great Seal. King James decided to use the Privy Seal as his means of obtaining money when Commons turned down his demands.

It was now 1606—the year the Virginia Company of London was formally chartered to found colonies in America. John Bates, a strong-willed and independent-minded merchant, refused to pay over the funds required of him under the Privy Seal. No money was owed to the government, he declared, unless authorized by Parliament. The case was tried in the Exchequer Court, where the judges were in sympathy with the crown. Predictably, Bates lost his case, and his freedom as well.

Commons and the king looked for a compromise after that case. Known as the Great Contract, it would have insured the king a yearly grant of 200,000 £ if he gave up the feudal powers of the Privy Seal. The arrangement was never agreed to, however, and James found that except in cases where money was needed in vast amounts, he could manage to get along without Parliament. The most important result of this struggle was that all parties in England now became aware of the constitutional issues at stake in turning to Magna Carta.

The first of the Stuart kings, James I, died in 1625 leaving the throne to his son Charles I. James had managed to keep the kingdom fairly peaceful and to squeeze out enough money by his feudal rights to avoid a final, all-out test of wills with the House of Commons.

For Charles I, however, the story was different. He was a shy young man who had not expected to come to the throne until his older brother died unexpectedly in 1612. The second son of the Stuart kings lacked the assurance that his father had gained from his years as king of the Scots. In such a hesitant monarch, the strong-minded Puritan politicians in the House of Commons saw the chance they had long been waiting for. A long drawn out war with Spain was becoming more and more expensive, so the new king would almost at once have to turn to Parliament for financial aid. The Commons intended to use its control over money to bargain with the crown.

A bitter division developed at once. The first two parliaments refused to consider the king's money requests unless their long list of reform proposals was first considered—and Charles dissolved both sessions. Unwisely, the king decided that he could turn to his father's tactic of Privy Seal requisitions for money. But James I had commanded his subjects to give "voluntarily" too often. They were not ready to give so freely to the new king. And besides, the war was forcing Charles to demand a particularly large sum.

Now the king made things worse by resorting to another ancient practice of putting a special tax on "tonnage and poundage" of exports and imports. This was followed, in September 1626, with the crudest device of all—a forced loan. Charles compelled his subjects to lend money to the crown with only his promise to repay in the indefinite future. Many persons refused to pay the loan and were arrested. Five defendants were prominent members of the Commons—John

Corbet, Thomas Darnel, Walter Earl, Edmond Hampden, and John Heveningham. They tried to prove their arrest was illegal by suing for a writ of habeas corpus (the right of a citizen to protect himself from illegal arrest).

The *Five Knights' Case,* or *Darnel's Case,* as it was also known, was a public test of the right of the subject to be free from arbitrary arrest. Counsel for the defense argued that the arrests without the filing of formal charges were in violation of Chapter 29 of Magna Carta, which stated that the subject could not be deprived of his liberty without due process of law. The crown counsel answered that the chapter did not apply to matters of national emergency. Arrests to stop plotting and treason were necessary without regard to the individual's rights. The chief flaw in the argument was that no one had been accused of conspiracy in this case. But the court returned the knights to prison without granting their petition. The kingdom rocked with the accusation that the judges had refused to enforce a guarantee of the ancient constitution.

The unpopular war with Spain presented another grievance. This was the practice of quartering troops in private homes, on the claim that the government lacked the money to pay for public lodging. The invasion of privacy, petty thefts and conflicts between the soldiers and the householders raised another storm of protest in the realm.

When the Parliament of 1628 was summoned, the members of Commons were aflame with resentment at the actions of the crown. Sir Benjamin Rudyard declared: "For mine own part, I shall be very glad to see that old decrepit law, *Magna Carta,* which hath been kept so long, and lien bed-rid, as it were, I shall be glad to see it walk abroad again with new vigour and lustre, . . . questionless it will be a great heartening to all the People."

John Glanville spoke in like vein about "the good old statute called Magna Carta, which declareth and confirmeth the ancient Common Law of the Liberties of England." But the dominating figure of this session was the aged Coke. He drafted the Petition of Right and called upon the Commons to stand firm as never before on the constitution. He rejected the reasoning of the court in the *Five Knights' Case;* "sovereign power is no Parliamentary word," he said, for "Magna Carta and all our statutes . . . are absolute without any saving of sovereign power."

Charles demanded that Parliament and the courts recognize the ancient prerogative powers of the crown, and Coke finally warned: "take we heed what we yield unto—Magna Carta is such a Fellow, he will have no Sovereign." Upon such ringing words, a majority in both houses was finally swung against the crown, and the Petition of Right was presented to Charles for his assent. The document condemned the forced loans, the denial of habeas corpus in cases of men seized for refusing to pay the loans, the quartering of troops in private homes, and the trial of defendants in these cases without common law safeguards.

*And where also by the statute called* THE GREAT CHARTER OF THE LIBERTIES OF ENGLAND, *it is declared and enacted, That no freeman shall be taken or imprisoned, or be disseized of his freehold or liberties, . . . but by the lawful judgment of his peers, or by the law of the land,*

the Petition declared, the crown must recognize that from the beginning of English law limits had been drawn on the feudal power of the monarch.

Charles tried to avoid a showdown by keeping his answer vague. He approved the petition thus making it law by stating that he found his subjects' liberty to be an obligation of the crown of the same weight as the king's prerogatives. It was an answer obviously composed by the crown attorneys, and it did not fool a lawyer as expert as Coke. The obligation of

Magna Carta was in no sense equal to the prerogative—it was *superior* to it. The Commons insisted upon this, and reluctantly Charles finally approved the document in the ancient formula: *Soit droit fait comme est desire* (Let the law be as is desired).

The Petition of Right was a major political and legal victory for free government. It was, as time would tell, unenforceable in its own right—who, after all, could go against the king without being in rebellion? But it would also be true that rebellion would be the final answer when the king refused to abide by the law. Charles did indeed ignore the Petition in the years that followed. But the Commons had written the proposition into the law of the land. Now it had a case for the legality of charging the king with violating the law.

Most important, by ratifying the Petition, the crown was ratifying Coke's own interpretation of the meaning of Chapter 29 of the Magna Carta. This interpretation took a good deal of liberty with historical fact. Even if the "due process" idea in this chapter were seen as simply a more developed version of what it meant in 1215, Coke was on shaky ground. He argued that all men in England had always accepted the Great Charter as controlling law, but history showed this not to be true. In the Wars of the Roses, for instance, no one would seriously have considered the argument.

But Coke, who had spent a lifetime studying ancient law reports and early statutes, was building a fundamental constitutional philosophy for the modern age. Since James I had forced him from the bench he had been at work on a monumental study of English law, the first volume of which—the famous *Coke on Littleton*—was soon to appear. It was known that the second volume would be devoted entirely to Magna Carta, the Confirmation of Edward I, and related medieval statutes. Having seen the effect of one chapter of the Great Charter upon the kingdom, Charles did not care to see a treatise on the whole document become ammunition for the rising democratic movement. Coke was considered "too great an oracle amongst the people," and a treatise on Magna Carta, if it was as convincing as his first volume, would be too much. In 1631, two years before Coke's death, his manuscripts were seized on the king's order and locked in the Tower of London.

It was twelve years before another parliament was summoned. And that one had members who complained loudly of Charles' failure to honor the Petition of Right and the general principle of the Great Charter. It was dismissed in a matter of weeks. But the king had all but run through his resources, having wasted money on a series of unsuccessful "police actions" in Scotland. This and his harsh treatment of Puritan preachers made it likely the House of Commons would take extreme action. In the winter of 1641, another parliament was called. It would not be dismissed until Charles was executed and the "Lord Protector," Oliver Cromwell, decided that he could run a dictatorship better without it.

By the following fall, both the crown and Parliament had raised armies for their respective causes. As Charles saw it, the demands of the Commons meant the destruction of the throne, or at least a curtailing of its power so that it was almost helpless. As the zealous Puritans saw it, the constitution—its ancient principle embodied in the Great Charter, its new statement in the Petition of Right—was henceforth the rule to which all functions of government must conform. Parliament was to be permitted to meet regularly, to be its own judge of when to close each session; its members were to be safe from arrest while performing their duties; and all matters of state were to be proper subjects for its debates.

The Commons then secured the release of Coke's manuscript on Magna Carta from the Tower of London, and in early 1642 it was published. The following year two other books appeared, expanding the thesis in Coke's volume. One was William Prynne's *Soveraigne Power of Parliament and*

*Kingdom* (not *the king*), and the other a manuscript by an anonymous prisoner in Bridewell Prison, *Brief Collections Out of Magna Carta; or, The Knowne Good Old Laws of England.* The developing conflict had aroused national "constitution consciousness" between Parliament and the royalists.

When the conflict finally erupted into war, Charles was at a disadvantage. He was cut off from the main cities, he had only a small band of trained fighters on his side, and the little money he had would soon be gone. Parliament's troops held the south and east of England—and with the Royal Navy switching to their side, they had the ships to keep foreign aid from getting through to the crown. Yet because the Parliamentary army was run by committee, a plan which was not very practical, and because Charles' military commanders were expert, the king was not defeated for four years. Finally, in 1646, Parliament won the battle of Marston Moor in the north of England and the king was taken prisoner by the Puritans.

Most members of Parliament fought the civil war to make the king admit Parliament's supremacy. But Charles still hoped matters would turn in his favor. He escaped in 1648 and a second war broke out. This time, when he was again taken prisoner, more extreme elements—Oliver Cromwell and his army of Roundheads—were in control of Parliament's forces. They demanded that the king be tried for high treason in making war on his own subjects. The king was speedily condemned and executed, and the Puritans proclaimed the monarchy abolished—along with the House of Lords. The House of Commons had thus emerged as the master of the kingdom.

But Scotland was not ready to follow the example of the radicals in London. It was announced that on New Year's Day, 1651, Charles II would be crowned in Edinburgh. Cromwell marched on Scotland and managed to scatter the royalists. Charles himself escaped to the Continent where he remained for the next ten years until the fury of the revolution had waned. For in the process of destroying the supremacy of the throne, the reform movement of Puritanism in time would destroy itself. Cromwell's self-righteousness very quickly passed into dictatorship, and he found the one-house Parliaments of 1655 and 1658 to be just as stubborn with him as they had been with the king.

Above all, the Puritan government failed because it did not practice the very principles of the modern constitution that it had advocated in its case against the crown. Puritanism, once it was in power, became an austere way of life, politically as well as theologically. But the rising middle classes in England were seeking freedom in both areas. The Commonwealth did not prove to be a republic. It showed only that government by committee could lead to government by one man—a dictatorship by a commoner instead of by a king.

There would be more disastrous experience with Stuart rulers, and another revolution before the English people were ready to form a workable constitutional democracy within the framework of a monarchy. What was taking place in England in the seventeenth century had occurred nowhere before in human history. Not even the democracy of ancient Greece, the government of the Roman Republic or the Venetian Republic of Renaissance times had really reached the ideal of a representative legislature to which the rulers would be accountable. In the end there always had been a strong man who made the final decisions.

The barons at Runnymede had thought of keeping the right to rebel as a means of controlling King John. And Stephen Langton, for all his foresight, could not think of a better alternative. Edward I had made the laws during his reign; Parliament was responsible only for filling in the details. A century and a half later, the Tudors had almost as much control over Parliament. Finally, when Parliament itself overthrew the throne and controlled the country, it produced remarkably little beneficial legislation. There were a number of reasons for its failures but the most important was that the revolutionaries had not understood the need for a system of checks and balances for democracy.

Oliver Cromwell died in 1658, and under the administration of his son Richard things went from bad to worse. The collapse of the so-called Commonwealth was only a matter of time. Charles II, waiting hopefully in Holland, sent a message of peace to Parliament in which he renounced the royal feudal prerogative. The House of Commons, which had been the only house of Parliament for years, prepared the way for a return to monarchy by restoring the House of Lords to its place in Parliament. They then invited the military governor of Scotland, General George Monck, to restore order in the realm and escort the new King Charles II to the throne. In May 1660, the Puritan Commonwealth came to a drab end.

During his twenty-five years on the throne, Charles II was tactful in bringing back the royalist institutions, and for the most part accepted the proposals of Parliament. One of the first parliamentary acts during this period of the Restoration of the Crown was a statute that wiped out a large number of feudal rights. Now this generation of Stuarts could not base a claim to prerogative on the outmoded practices of the past. In parliamentary government, a law is in force until repealed by a later law, or unless it was temporary to begin with. English government has therefore needed houscleaning from time to time by repealing "sleeping statutes."

The gradual return of royal authority led eventually to more complaints that the crown was not protecting the subjects' rights. Lord Clarendon, the chief minister of Charles II, was much too sensitive to criticisms of the crown. To avoid granting political enemies their rights of habeas corpus he hit upon the device of arresting political enemies and shipping them to islands outside of England. This was illegal, for the king's

subjects had those rights guaranteed in the great Petition of 1628. For these arbitrary acts, Clarendon was impeached in 1667, and bills were introduced into the House of Commons seeking to strengthen still further the habeas corpus privilege.

It was not until 1679, however, that the definitive Habeas Corpus Act—the second of the four fundamentals of the modern English constitution—was perfected by Parliament. Coke had insisted—not very accurately—that habeas corpus had been known from Magna Carta. The Tudors had revived it in something like its modern use. But it was meant then to be used by the common law courts to take cases and defendants away from the special prerogative courts of Elizabeth I. It was not until the *Five Knights' Case* that it had been urged as a "writ of right" for all Englishmen.

The court in the Knights' case had declared that the procedure of Chapter 39 did not apply to the jailing of persons ordered by special command of the king. That decision was supposed to be overruled by Chapter 29 of Magna Carta in the Petition of Right, but the behavior of both Charles I and II had tended to make the provision ineffective. Parliament now ruled in unmistakable terms that the writ was to be honored universally. Any court in the English dominions was charged with the responsibility of issuing a habeas corpus writ and compelling the officers in charge of the jail to deliver the prisoner to the court without delay.

In 1685 Charles II died and his brother ascended the throne as James II. James would have a short tenure. His was the least remarkable of the Stuart reigns except that the king did have a truly remarkable power to infuriate his subjects. The key issues turned, as they had for most of the century, on religious questions that were really forms of political questions. Both Charles and James were devoted Roman Catholics, while Parliament, not wanting to encourage separate dissenting Protestant groups, had insisted that all holders of office in the realm should be members of the Anglican church.

Charles had made a major policy error in passing a "Declaration of Indulgence," which sought to give equal civil rights to all Catholics and Protestants. This had resulted in an outcry because the Declaration suspended the operation of nearly forty acts of Parliament. But James did the same thing on a more monumental scale. He issued "Declarations" that extended freedom of public worship to Catholics and Protestants as well as to the Anglicans. This sounds fair and just to modern ears, but Parliament was furious. It had struggled long to keep the crown under the authority of the law. For the King to nullify an act of Parliament was to invade the lawmaking prerogative of the legislature. For Parliament to allow this would be to watch all the gains of sixty years disappear. If the king could get away with this, he would feel free in the future to suspend any law for any purpose he chose.

Charles had retreated from his position on the "Declaration of Indulgence." James, however, had no intention of backing down as his brother had done. He was obsessed with the idea of enabling his fellow Catholics to hold public office. He did not see that by doing this he was disregarding acts of Parliament. He directed that the Declarations of Indulgence be read in all Anglican cathedrals. But seven bishops refused to do so on the ground that the Declarations were in violation of acts of Parliament. The bishops petitioned the crown for a consideration of their reasons, but the petitions themselves were called treasonous and made the basis of criminal charges. Before a court packed with royalist judges, a jury returned verdicts of not guilty. With the *Case of the Seven Bishops,* the stage was set for another Revolution.

This was known as the "Glorious Revolution." It was swift, all but bloodless, and kept the gains of the Restoration and the Parliamentary victories of the century. Indeed, with the overthrow of James II in 1688, the solution of the problem of constitutional government at last was at hand.

William of Orange was the son-in-law of James II, having

married his elder daughter Mary. As James' government collapsed, there were hasty exchanges of messages between William and Mary in Europe and the leaders of Parliament seeking to avoid a new civil war. These resulted in assurances from the prince and princess that they would accept any constitutional limitation that Parliament saw fit to devise. So ineffectual was James II that after taking away his crown Parliament did not even consider killing him as it had his father. He was allowed to leave the realm forever.

The third and climactic element in the modern English constitution—the Bill of Rights—was now to be drafted in 1688. Its opening section was deliberately copied in the opening of the Declaration of Independence of the United States eighty-six years later: The "late King James the Second, . . . did endeavor to subvert . . . the laws and liberties of this kingdom" was a phrase nearly identical in meaning to the Declaration's words: "The history of the present King of Great Britain is a history of repeated injuries and usurpations, all having in direct object the establishment of an absolute tyranny over these states." A bill of particular complaints followed in each case.

Then came a catalog of the rights of the English people— rights to which Americans of 1776 would appeal in their Declaration of Independence and that later would be found in the first ten Amendments to the American Constitution. The similarity in principle was so striking that the Amendments immediately came to be called the American Bill of Rights. William III and Mary II accepted the English Bill of Rights as the rights of their subjects and thereby limited their authority as monarchs. Now at last the principle of Chapter 29 of the Magna Carta had become a reality and a government of free men a practical possibility.

# 6

# Cornerstone of the
# American Constitution

IN October 1774, representatives from England's thirteen American colonies met at the first Continental Congress in Philadelphia. Feeling strongly about the tyranny of King George III, the Congress published a declaration of basic rights that they insisted were guaranteed to "the inhabitants of the English colonies in North-America, by the immutable laws of nature, the principles of the English constitution, and the several charters of compacts" granted to the colonies or drafted by them. The delegates to the Congress stated that they were preparing the petition "as Englishmen, their ancestors in like cases have usually done, for asserting and vindicating their rights and liberties."

Among the ten resolutions adopted by the Congress was the claim "that our ancestors, who first settled these colonies, were at the time of their emigration from the mother country, entitled to all the rights, liberties and immunities of free and natural-born subjects, within the realm of England." This was, in fact, almost the identical language of the first charter granted to the Virginia Company in 1606. And while a new and different concept of colonial rights had developed in England in the following years, the next resolution of the Congress specifically rejected it by declaring "that by such emigration they by no means forfeited, surrendered or lost any of those rights, but that they were, and their descendants now are, entitled to the exercise and enjoyment of all such of them, as their local and other circumstances enable them to exercise and enjoy."

The rest of the resolutions enumerated the rights the colonists felt to be theirs. They were entitled to local self-government, to "the common law of England, and more especially to the great and inestimable privilege of being tried by their peers [in their own colonies] according to the course of that law," to the benefit of parliamentary laws up to the time of colonization, to special privileges contained in their charters.

The declaration made at Philadelphia clearly showed that the American colonists were well aware of the constitutional developments in England during the past century, and they assumed that as Englishmen they were entitled to the benefit of these developments wherever the English flag was carried. They specifically cited the right of trial by peers under due process of law from Magna Carta; the privilege of being exempt from the quartering of soldiers in private homes, from the Petition of Right; security of person and property guaranteed by the Habeas Corpus Act; and the right of peaceable assembly and petition as stated in the Bill of Rights.

Parliament and the administrators of overseas colonies did not accept the view that the constitution followed the flag. And this was the ultimate root of the struggle between the colonies and the crown. "Did English subjects leave the mother country as free men and land in an English colony as second-class citizens?" asked James Wilson, a Scottish emigrant who would one day be a Justice of the Supreme Court. Ten years earlier Benjamin Franklin had been a member of a commission from the colonies protesting the Stamp Act, which seemed unfair taxation to the colonists. He told a committee of the

House of Commons that the Stamp Act was a tax measure enacted by a government in which the colonists had no voice and that it violated another provision of the Petition of Right. At almost the same time, Thomas Pownall, a former governor of Massachusetts Bay Colony, wrote that a colony could not be limited to rights "within a narrower scale than the subject is entitled to, by the Great Charter of England."

The colonists showed that they were just as stubborn in sticking to their rights as their countrymen at home. From the beginning it had been so; the Massachusetts Body of Liberties in 1641 had incorporated Chapter 29 of Magna Carta, as had the Connecticut Code of 1650 and the New York Charter of Liberties in 1683. Four years later, William Penn published in Philadelphia, his City of Brotherly Love, a tract under the tidy title of *The Excellent Privilege of Liberty & Property; Being the British Right of the Free-Born Subjects of England.* This included the complete text of the Great Charter and the Confirmation of Edward I among other basic documents for the colony of Pennsylvania. In the Carolina colonies, local assembly acts in 1712 and 1715 built into the law the constitutional statutes of the English Revolution itself.

Ministers in London advised the crown to veto the New York and Carolina colonial acts. But there were more and more colonial declarations that such denials went against the English constitution. Most of the arguments leading to the American Revolution were the same arguments as those between the leaders of Parliament and the Stuarts in the seventeenth century.

On July 6, 1775, the next session of the Continental Congress complained that although George III had "graciously received" the declarations of the previous October, nothing had come of them. Instead, it was formally stated at the second Philadelphia meeting that the declarations had been "huddled into both houses among a bundle of American papers, and there neglected" by Parliament. The Congress admitted that "an illustrious band of the most distinguished peers, and commoners, who nobly and strenuously asserted the justice of our cause" had sought in vain for a serious consideration of the 1774 resolutions. It declared that it had been forced to take up arms against the armies of occupation that Parliament had sent in answer to their petition.

While both sides stuck to their positions, the crisis moved swiftly in the spring of 1776 to a revolution based upon a constitutional claim. In the American Declaration of Independence declared on July 4, 1776, the parallels between the case against George III and the guarantees of the Petition of 1628 and the Bill of Rights of 1688 were remarkable: George III, like James II, was charged with having "dissolved Representative Houses repeatedly," levying arbitrary taxes and suspending colonial laws—contrary to the clear provisions in the Bill of Rights stating that elected legislatures "ought to be held frequently," that "levying money . . . without grant of parliament . . . is illegal," as was "the pretended power of suspending of laws."

Thus the colonists became revolutionists and citizens of a new republic. During all that time they insisted on the rights guaranteed by the English constitution. That constitution, said Thomas Jefferson after independence, was the finest document devised by free men—so long as it was properly administered and universally guaranteed! His main objection to the American Constitution drafted in the summer of 1787 was based on the need for proper administration and guarantees of rights. The Constitution must be amended, he said, for power in government would always be a dangerous temptation to abuse. Nothing less than a Bill of Rights had sufficed for the English people a century before, and nothing less was required for the new Constitution of the United States.

The new state constitutions were adopted by most of the

original colonies after the Declaration of Independence. They incorporated the English Bill of Rights, and in many cases enlarged upon it. Virginia's first state constitution was drawn up several weeks before the Declaration of Independence. It contained sixteen provisions in its bill of rights drawn (through the work of Jefferson and George Mason) from the English statute and the writings of John Locke. The constitutions of Pennsylvania and Delaware, a few weeks later, were substantially the same as Virginia's. Those of Maryland and North Carolina used the wording of many specific Parliamentary statutes on the subject of rights of individuals. The constitution of Massachusetts, while referring to the provisions in English law, took the position that all power came from the people of the commonwealth itself, and that the people themselves were the sovereigns in the new nation.

To many, a Bill of Rights seemed an essential part of any constitution. But to others, it seemed unnecessary. They argued that the English Bill of Rights was a protection against the crown and since the American people themselves were sovereigns in their own country, they needed no such protections.

However, those men who feared an abuse of power by a strong government won the day.

Accordingly, the first Congress meeting under the Constitution received many proposals for inclusion in a Bill of Rights. Twelve of these were approved by the Congress and submitted to the people for their approval. Ten were adopted as amendments to the Constitution and they came to be known as the American Bill of Rights. For the most part, they were modeled after the state constitutional bills adopted during the Revolution, but through these documents they traced most of their principles directly back to the English constitution.

To illustrate this heritage, one need only compare specific clauses in the first ten Amendments and the similar clauses in various English sources:

*Amendment 1:* "Congress shall make no law . . . abridging . . . the right of the people peaceably to assemble, and to petition the government for a redress of grievances."

*Bill of Rights 5:* "That it is the right of the subjects to petition the King, and all commitments and prosecutions for such petitioning are illegal."

*Amendment 2:* ". . . the right of the people to keep and bear arms shall not be infringed."

*Bill of Rights 7:* "That the subjects . . . may have arms for their defense suitable to their conditions, and as allowed by law."

*Amendment 3:* "No soldier shall . . . be quartered in any house without the consent of the owner. . . ."

*Petition of Right 4 and 10:* "And whereas of late great companies of soldiers and mariners have been dispersed . . . and the inhabitants against their wills have been compelled to receive them into their houses, . . . [Parliament prays] that your Majesty would be pleased to remove the said soldiers and mariners, and that your people may not be so burdened in time to come . . ."

*Amendment 5:* "No person shall be held to answer for a capital or otherwise infamous crime, . . . nor to be deprived of life, liberty, or property, without due process of law . . ."

*Magna Carta, Ch. 29:** "No freeman shall be taken, imprisoned, disseized, . . . or in any way destroyed, nor will we . . . prosecute him, except . . . by the law of the land."

*Amendment 5:* ". . . nor shall private property be taken for public use, without just compensation."

*Magna Carta, Ch. 19:* "No constable or other bailiff of ours shall take anyone's grain or other chattels . . . without immediately paying for them in money . . ."

*Amendment 6:* "In all criminal prosecutions the accused shall enjoy the right to a speedy and public trial, by an impartial

* See also Petition of Right 3.

jury of the state and district wherein the crime shall have been committed . . ."

*Magna Carta, Ch. 14:* "A freeman shall not be [prosecuted] . . . except by the oaths of lawful men of the neighborhood. . . ."

*Amendment 8:* "Excessive bail shall not be required, nor excessive fines imposed, nor cruel and unusual punishments inflicted."

*Bill of Rights 10:* "That excessive bail ought not to be required, nor excessive fines imposed; nor cruel and unusual punishments inflicted."

And so the Great Charter of 1215 had followed English constitutional ideas, if not the English flag, to the New World. And where it was not used specifically in the American Bill of Rights, it had prepared the way, in the parliamentary arguments of the seventeenth century, for the other elements of the English constitution that were included in the first Amendments to the American Constitution.

The concept of due process is the insistence that the state can deal with the life, liberty and property of the individual only if the individual can defend himself and his property against arbitrary state action. This has been the taproot of American constitutional thought. The colonists had themselves learned the evils of arbitrary government. And they could look at the history of England since Runnymede to strengthen their belief that the arbitrary acts were evil. "As to the words from Magna Carta," declared Supreme Court Justice William Johnson in the early nineteenth century, "after volumes spoken and written with a view to their exposition, the good sense of mankind has at length settled down to this: that they were intended to secure the individual from the arbitrary exercise of the powers of government, unrestrained by the established principles of private right and distributive justice."

In 1868 the Fourteenth Amendment to the Constitution

was enacted. It provided that "No State shall . . . deprive any person of life, liberty or property without due process of law." The concept had now broadened to include restraints upon state as well as national government in its dealings with the individual. As new states were created in the nineteenth and twentieth centuries, · their constitutions preserved the doctrine as well. In the mid-Pacific Ocean, the fiftieth state of Hawaii repeated it in 1959, seven and a half centuries after King John and the barons met at Runnymede.

The "good sense of mankind," in Justice Johnson's phrase, has also made another part of Magna Carta—as Lord Coke argued it—a basic feature of American constitutional law. This is the guarantee of the "great writ" of habeas corpus as fundamental in due process of law itself. Again, in his eagerness to show that the Great Charter was the source of the citizens' fundamental rights, Coke had fallen into error. But his overly strong claim for the ancient constitution had been approved by men of his own time and so made a valid part of the modern constitution. Coke had argued that the writ of habeas corpus could force courts to examine the reasons and lawfulness of an individual's being held in jail and make certain that he was released until he could have a trial under reasonable conditions.

The original understanding of habeas corpus had not been that. Rather, it had been a way to force the individual to show up in court to have his case tried. In Tudor times it had allowed the common law courts to transfer custody of a defendant from the special courts to their own jurisdiction. But since the *Five Knights' Case* had proved a victory against the abuses of James I and Charles I, it was generally held by supporters of the English Revolution that government should be forced to account for the individuals it took into custody, and to do so promptly with valid legal grounds.

Coke finished the treatise on the Great Charter and it was

published after his death in the second volume of his *Institutes*. There he had written: "By these writs, it manifestly appeareth, that no men ought to be imprisoned, but for some certain cause; and . . . that cause must be showed; for otherwise how can the court take order therein according to law?"

Coke's claims for habeas corpus were stoutly seconded by a friend and contemporary, John Selden, one of the attorneys for the defense in the *Five Knights' Case*. In the process, Selden captured the essence of a democratic government. If the meaning of the words "by the law of the land" meant only "according to law," Selden told the court, the Great Charter had accomplished nothing. Dictatorships, as readily as democracies, could say that they followed the *form* of the law. But only democracies, and never dictatorships, could claim to rule within the spirit of the law. In this sense, the meaning of the Great Charter in 1215 was the same as in the seventeenth —or the twentieth—centuries. To King John, to the Stuart monarchs, to George III and to the state and national governments in the United States, the fundamental rule in Magna Carta was that the ruler as well as the ruled had to be *under* the law.

This was the meaning of due process. And this was why the English and American constitution-makers of the seventeenth and eighteenth centuries felt that the liberty of individuals insured by habeas corpus was part of the concept of due process. It was considered so important by the men at the Constitutional Convention of 1787 that it was written into the first Article of the Constitution: "The privilege of the Writ of Habeas Corpus shall not be suspended, unless when in cases of rebellion or invasion if the public safety may require it."

It was not until the American Civil War in the 1860s that the "great writ" became as important in American law as it had become in England during the civil wars and the "Glorious Revolution" of the Stuart reigns. Believing that the clause in the Constitution permitted the President to suspend the writ in time of rebellion, Abraham Lincoln sent an order to various military commanders announcing a suspension of Habeas Corpus. Chief Justice Roger B. Taney reviewed a case challenging the President's order. He argued that only Congress could suspend the writ because, among other reasons, the language in the Constitution appeared in the Article on legislative powers.

Lincoln ignored the Supreme Court ruling, but Congress eventually enacted a statute anyway, which suspended the writ for the duration of the war. In the Reconstruction period after the Civil War, another habeas corpus appeal was presented by a Mississippi editor, William H. McCardle, to force his release from arbitrary arrest by military authorities. Before the Supreme Court could answer the question, Congress took it from the court's jurisdiction—but not before the military authorities themselves had agreed to obey the writ. A lower Federal court had issued it pursuant to "the great American . . . charter of personal liberty."

Having seen the importance of habeas corpus in matters of personal liberty, Congress enacted, in 1867, a law authorizing all Federal courts to issue the writ "in all cases where any person may be restrained of his or her liberty in violation of the Constitution." Almost two centuries after the Habeas Corpus Act of the English constitution, the language that sprang in spirit if not (as Coke and Selden had claimed) in fact from Magna Carta was written into American law.

Time and changing court opinions made the great writ applicable to a broader and broader variety of cases. As the Federal courts, in the mid-twentieth century, began to look more carefully at state criminal procedure, anything that was found to have denied due process of law to the defendant might become the basis for a habeas corpus petition in the Federal courts. The original understanding was that the writ forced courts—or any government agency—to bring forth a prisoner and decide the charges against him and the legality of his imprisonment before trial. Now it was broadened to a point where the writ could force the government to show that the trial itself had been fair and that the defendant's imprisonment after conviction was legal.

This change in judicial thought concerning habeas corpus is important to the story of Magna Carta. It shows how the general ideas in the Great Charter came to have a new and more advanced meaning in the New World to which they were transported. Just as the English Revolution ratified Coke's argument about the meaning of Magna Carta, so the American Revolution ratified the colonists' argument that the "rights of Englishmen" had come with them across the ocean.

Once the ideas had crossed the ocean, they took on meanings that local circumstances required. In the nineteenth century, industry and big business wanted the protection of due process to keep state governments from trying to control their size by law. In this same period, a Reconstruction Congress strengthened the habeas corpus process as a way to keep states from denying rights to slaves freed after the Civil War. In the twentieth century, due process was interpreted as strengthening, not holding back, the power of the government to regulate business. Habeas corpus became a guarantee of the individual's rights at every stage in government proceedings against him.

This change was built into the idea of the Great Charter itself. As it had changed to fit new conditions over the centuries, so it would continue to change if it was to be a vital force in the future. In the constitutional law of the 1960s, the rights of the individual were defined in terms of limits on the state's actions and in terms of responsibilities of the state to help the individual gain his rights. A monumental decision by the Supreme Court of the United States in 1963 illustrated this development.

Clarence Gideon was a middle-aged Florida man who had been in and out of jails and prisons during much of his adult life. He had been arrested on a charge of entering a poolroom to commit robbery. When his case came up for trial he asked the Florida court to appoint an attorney to defend him. The judge told Gideon that under Florida law the court was not required to provide a lawyer in any case except those involving a capital charge, such as murder. Gideon, who claimed that the Constitution guaranteed him this right of legal counsel, was convicted and sentenced to the Florida penitentiary.

A hand-written petition for habeas corpus went from Gideon's prison to the Supreme Court, the highest court in the land. The court appointed one of the ablest attorneys in the District of Columbia—Abe Fortas, later himself a Justice of the Court—as counsel for this obscure defendant. Gideon, at the time of his trial, had been wrong about the right of any defendant to a lawyer if he could not afford to hire one. But on the basis of Fortas' strong argument, which summed up many years of criticism of the existing rule, the Supreme Court overturned the previous law and agreed that Gideon was entitled to legal counsel.

There is no way to have equal justice, said Justice Hugo Black in a similar case, where a man's right to have trained lawyers represent him at his trial or in a review of his case depends on whether or not he can afford a lawyer. The principle of a general "right to counsel" is another extension of the basic principle of the Great Charter itself. If the barons at Runnymede were entitled to their feudal rights against the paramount lord, then all men were ultimately entitled to their rights against the government. Men who can afford to hire a lawyer are usually able to protect the rights to which they are entitled. Other men may not have the money for a lawyer, but they still do have the right to be protected.

The case of *Gideon v. Wainwright* has become one of the landmark decisions in the history of human freedom. It is true that Gideon was prosecuted when there was reasonable ground for accusing him, but the state should not have been permitted to prosecute until the defendant was given means for making his defense. In a complex modern society, this involves the services of a trained attorney, and if the individual cannot afford to retain one it is now the responsibility of the state to provide one for him. While anyone may defend himself, no one who knows what it involved would attempt to do so. As Fortas pointed out in his brief for Gideon, even skilled criminal lawyers if made defendants in certain cases will engage other attorneys to conduct their defenses. Indeed, Gideon, who was convicted when he carried on his own defense, won an acquittal when court-appointed counsel defended him in a second trial.

In a society that is becoming more cosmopolitan and economically centralized, there is more and more danger that the voice of the individual may be drowned out in the uproar of great affairs. The Supreme Court has insisted in recent years that the voice of the individual be heard. The impersonal force of institutional government must be kept from overriding the relatively small and relatively insignificant. No one may be deprived of life, liberty, or property without due process of law.

Thus the struggle that was first dramatized at Runnymede in 1215—although it had been going on long before—continues today and will continue in the future. "The Petition of Right, like Magna Carta," wrote Justice Felix Frankfurter in 1953, "was the beginning, not the end, of a struggle for the principles it enunciated." In the constitutional framework of the United States, the emphasis on due process and habeas corpus is the most persuasive evidence that the fundamental concept in the Great Charter did indeed become the corner-stone of our own legal structure, and the democracy it protects.

# 7

# Magna Carta Today

THE original Charter of 1215 contained sixty-three chapters. By the definitive reissue of 1225, these had been reduced to thirty-seven. These continued in force—at least in name—until 1660. Then Parliament repealed the chapters relating to feudal tenures. In 1863 a number of other chapters considered out of date were also repealed. Parts of ten chapters of the Great Charter remain in force today in England. Like Magna Carta as a whole, they stand for a spirit of law rather than specific laws, and as such they will endure as long as there is an Anglo-American constitutional ideal.

It is worthwhile to consider the principles expressed in the surviving chapters. Of the ten, only the famous Chapter 29 has anything like the full force of law in the twentieth century. But the fact that Parliament has preserved the others as well shows that they stand for something important in the philosophy of freedom under representative government.

To see this significance is not always easy, since some of the surviving chapters seem trivial or obscure today. A brief explanation of each of these surviving chapters may therefore be helpful.

*Ch. 1. First, . . . that the English Church shall be free, and have all her rights and liberties inviolate.*

The principle of freedom for the "English Church" has meant a number of different things throughout English history. But it has never been the same principle as "non-establishment" of an official religion in the United States. In the thirteenth century, the opening chapter of Magna Carta meant, of course, something very different. In that time, long before Protestantism was dreamed of, freedom of religion for individuals had never been considered. Freedom for the church leaders and the clergy was the important thing, and the Magna Carta chapter was designed to point that out. In 1215, every person in Christendom was subject to two rules of law, one concerning a wide range of economic affairs and the other an equally wide range of personal affairs.

By the time of the Reformation, the principle meant something new. The established Church of England was now independent of the church in Rome. But the Tudors did not go far enough with their Anglican Church to suit the rising middle classes and their Puritan leaders. During the religious conflicts of the seventeenth century Chapter 1 would have been understood to mean that the Church of England should be free from Catholic form and faith.

The Toleration Acts of the Restoration brought some freedom of religious practices to Protestants, but the Catholics did not share in it. The firm commitment of the government to an Established Church, however, has made toleration of all religious beliefs the most accurate reading of the Great Charter chapter. The Roman Catholic Relief Act was passed in 1829, and other laws that recognized the church organization plans of Jews, Quakers, Unitarians and Protestant sects in general. Thus the Church in all its forms in England was freeing itself both from Rome and from supervision by the state.

The concept of government-approved religion was common

in the early days of the colonies as well. Massachusetts was a colony founded and controlled by Puritans. They were as harsh toward dissenters as the English church had been to the Puritans, when they had themselves been the dissenters. The New York Colony recognized the need for balancing its two groups of settlers and their religious interests. The Dutch Reformed Church and the Anglican Church were given equal recognition, but other groups were not given such freedom. Pennsylvania was a Quaker Commonwealth, and Virginia an Anglican one. Neither colony was happy about groups that did not agree with them. Maryland, founded by the Calvert family for Roman Catholic refugees, had a pioneering statute on freedom of religion. But later, when the Anglicans outnumbered the Roman Catholics, they gained in official power. Then oppression was once again the rule for Catholics.

Thomas Jefferson, with his famous Statute for Religious Freedom in Virginia, at last pointed the way toward the total separation of church and state, which became a cardinal principle of the American Constitution. Even so, it was a struggle to get the statute through the Virginia legislature. And other states were slow to follow Virginia's lead. One might even argue, in fact, that the proposition was in the First Amendment of the Constitution simply to guarantee freedom to discuss public issues, and not to guarantee freedom of doctrine.

A glance at the Amendment tends to support this view: "Congress shall make no law respecting an establishment of religion, or prohibiting the free exercise thereof," is the opening clause of the Amendment. The clause also deals with two other means of expression—speech and press, and assembly and petition. The opening proposition of the American Bill of Rights, in any event, was concerned with the various ways that citizens of the new nation could promote public discussion. Thus, the eighteenth-century view of the clause in the First Amendment was mostly a political one. But in the nineteenth century restraint placed solely on the national government was stressed because state laws laying burdens upon various religions were fairly common in this period.

It has only been in the mid-twentieth century that the Supreme Court—to the considerable shock of many persons—has carried the "anti-establishment" clause to its logical extreme. In a series of cases the Court declared that the clause in the First Amendment extended to the states through the Fourteenth. Thus it became unconstitutional to read the Bible or a special non-sectarian prayer in public schools supported by government funds. Some people protested against an "atheistic" legal doctrine. But what the Court really meant was simply that the clause against establishing an official religion or regulating the free exercise of religious belief meant that government-supported activities must be totally separate from religious activities.

Chapter 8 of Magna Carta states: *We, or our bailiffs, shall not seize any land or rent for any debt, so long as the present goods and chattels of the debtor suffice to pay the debt, and the debtor himself is ready to satisfy therefor.* This chapter is best understood in association with the opening clause of *Ch. 14. A freeman shall not be amerced for a small fault; but after the manner of the fault. . . .* Again, of course, modern thinking was different from the medieval. To the thirteenth century mind, these were simply safeguards against abuses in the system of land tenancies. The original purpose was to guard against too heavy punishments—debtors need pay only enough to satisfy the debt and no more, and no one should be forced to pay more than he deserved to pay in fines.

In the sense that "amercements"—payments by a person who was "in mercy" or at the mercy of his creditor—came to be equivalent to fines in a modern sense, the spirit of Chapter 14 is continued in the prohibition in the English and American Bills of Rights against "excessive fines." The two chapters have been kept in modern English constitutional law as the principle of restraint against arbitrary seizure of private property, or unreasonable demands for public payment, in cases of debts claims or criminal claims by the state.

The principle thus remains clear, but the application of it is flexible. No one has ever defined just how large a fine must be to be "excessive." The law protects in spirit rather than in particular.

The principle set out in these surviving chapters of Magna Carta, therefore, is a general one, "sleeping" as the British would describe it, but presumably ready to come into operation if the issue were to materialize.

Four other surviving chapters may be considered together, for the general principles they represent:

*Ch. 9. The City of London shall have all the old liberties and customs which it used to have. Moreover, we will and grant that all other cities, boroughs, towns . . . shall have all their liberties and customs.*

*Ch. 15. No town or freeman shall be compelled to make bridges . . .*

*Ch. 16. No riverbanks shall be put "in defense" . . .*

*Ch. 23. All [fishweirs] from henceforth shall be utterly put down . . .*

These chapters had specific and special meaning for the Middle Ages. London, with its charter dating from before the Conquest, and other cities and boroughs that had early charters, wanted to keep these privileges and exemptions from feudal law. The fishweirs that were the concern of Chapter 23 were a serious problem at that time. These contraptions for catching fish had permanent pilings that extended into England's principal rivers and became a serious hazard to boats on the river.

The "making of bridges" and the "defense" of riverbanks were another peculiarly medieval problem. Putting the bridges and the highways near them into repair was a local responsibility, but the sudden appearance of the traveling royal court in a locality might place an unreasonable burden on the local yeomen. More serious was the placing of areas of river bottom land "in defense" or "out of bounds" for a period in which the king might elect to enjoy falconry and other sport—even though the crops growing there might be ruined since the farmers could not tend crops on land that was out of bounds.

Of course, these particular problems covered in Chapters 15, 16, and 23 have become of no importance in modern times. They stand today as a symbol. Whether it be fishweirs or smokestacks of factories or noisy machinery, any nuisance that keeps other individuals from using or enjoying their own property or the public facilities must be controlled by the government. The general interest of the public as a whole is to be protected. Although we no longer have riverbanks "in defense," the government still cannot force the surrender of private premises for public use.

The local charter principle has remained essentially the same throughout the years. Local government, in fact, is largely based upon a charter granted to a municipality by a state government, and such charters today are as jealously preserved by modern cities and towns as were those of medieval England. The "home rule" movement in the United States between the 1870s and the late 1920s, which sought to strengthen local municipal charters against arbitrary encroachments by the superior government, acted in much the same spirit as did the burghers of London in 1215. The fact that the movement has since waned is largely a testimonial to the fact that the rights of local government are now almost universally recognized in the United States.

*Ch. 30. All merchants . . . shall have their safe and sure conduct to depart out of England, to come into . . . and go through England, as well by land as by water, to buy and sell without any manner of evil tolls . . .* This chapter may be taken to stand for the modern principle of freedom of trade between private parties who are from different countries. It was a particularly important concession in the thirteenth century when vague boundaries and allegiances made it difficult to establish the identity of foreigners, and when foreigners in turn might be subject to "evil tolls" or exorbitant excise taxes.

The beginning of the modern age of international trade, as well as of international law, was marked by the development of treaties "of friendship and commerce." These established the rights of foreign traders in the nations that drafted the treaties. Each country was now responsible for the safety and good treatment of the other country's traders or businessmen. A further provision of this chapter was that in case of war between the two countries each would treat the private citizens or traders "as our merchants be entreated there in the land making war against us." This led to the rule of international law providing for the interning of enemy aliens and the custody of their property until hostilities have ended.

*Ch. 37. And all these customs and liberties aforesaid, which we have granted to be held in this our realm, . . . we shall observe . . .* With this concluding chapter of Magna Carta, still preserved on the rolls of English law, we have a general policy statement. "All these customs and liberties" are more than the specific surviving chapters of the Great Charter. They include the political convictions of the English people evolved over seven and a half centuries since Runnymede—and many generations before that.

For in the final analysis, Magna Carta never declared anything new under the sun. It was a very practical restatement of what English freemen (as the term was then understood) had already come to recognize as elemental rights of an organized government. It survived because it was the most complete written description of these rights. It also was clear evidence that the crown recognized their existence and their obligation.

The nine surviving chapters—together with the famous

Chapter 29—reflect an attitude toward government. That attitude had been enlarged upon by men like Edward Coke and John Selden on the eve of the English Revolution. It was summarized in John Locke's famous essay on government after the "Glorious Revolution," and rephrased in its American context by men like Thomas Jefferson, George Mason, James Madison and Alexander Hamilton in the framing of the Declaration of Independence and the Constitution.

This attitude has broadened and changed with the centuries. Every English subject and every American citizen today considers himself a "freeman" who is owed the rights of the Great Charter. Just as important, the government and laws of these two great democracies also have as their basic premise the idea that all of their subjects or citizens are entitled to these rights equally. The Great Charter and the English and American constitutions are ideas that have changed with the times through the thirteenth, seventeenth, eighteenth and twentieth centuries. The paper on which they were written will eventually crumble; the convictions that they represent will live as long as men wish to be free.

# Appendix

# Magna

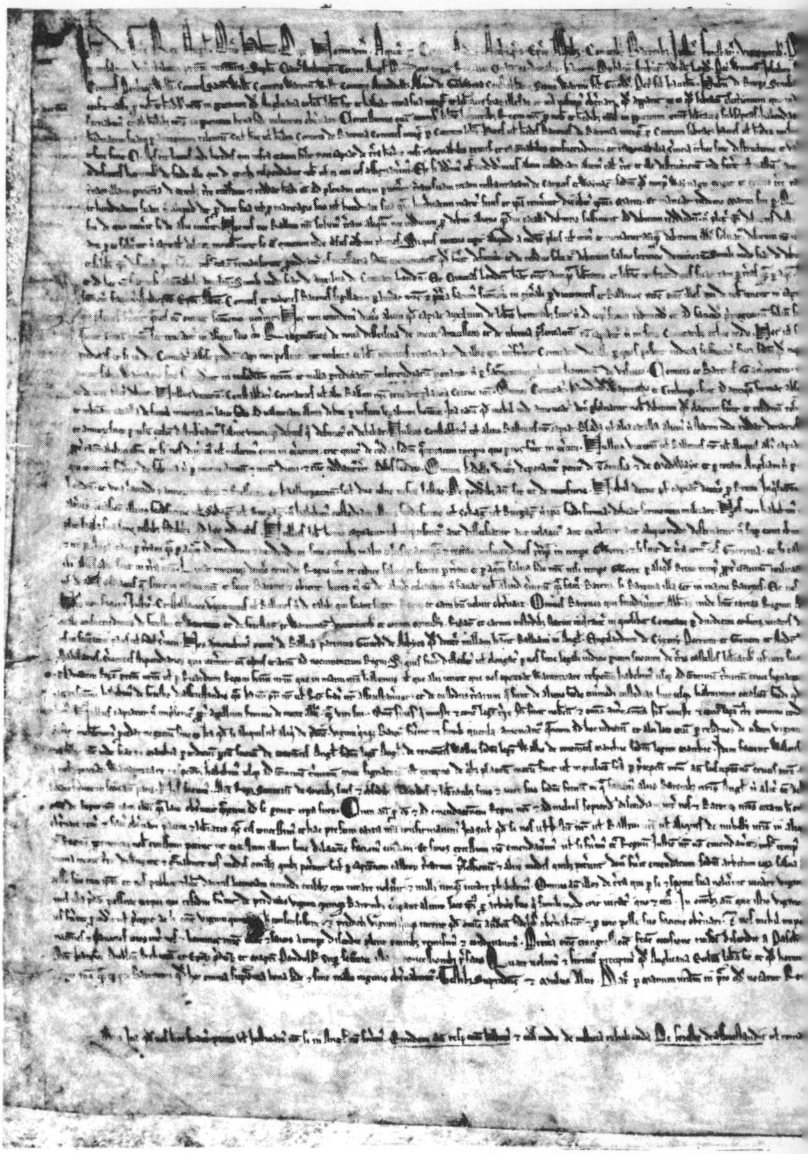

*Reproduced from an original in the*

# Carta

*British Museum (Cotton MS. Augustus ii. 106)*

# The Golden Passage

Sir Edward Coke (1552–1634) called this provision in Magna Carta "the golden passage" of English law. The "chapter" is still a living part of the English constitution, and its direct relation to the Constitution of the United States is illustrated by the parallel concepts in italics found in the examples reproduced below.

### MAGNA CARTA

#### Chapter 39

*No freeman shall be taken, imprisoned, disseised,* outlawed, *or in any way destroyed, nor will we* proceed against him or *prosecute him, except* by the lawful judgment of his peers, and *by the law of the land.*

### CONSTITUTION OF THE UNITED STATES

#### Amendment V

*No person shall be held to answer* for a capital, or otherwise infamous crime, unless on a presentment or indictment by a grand jury . . . , *nor shall any person . . . be deprived of life, liberty, or property, without due process of law . . .*

# Magna Carta

JOHN, by the grace of God King of England, Lord of Ireland, Duke of Normandy and Aquitaine, and Count of Anjou, to his archbishops, bishops, abbots, earls, barons, justices, foresters, sheriffs, stewards, servants, and to all his officials and loyal subjects, Greeting.

KNOW THAT BEFORE GOD, for the health of our soul and those of our ancestors and heirs, to the honour of God, the exaltation of the holy Church, and the better ordering of our kingdom, at the advice of our reverend fathers Stephen, archbishop of Canterbury, primate of all England, and cardinal of the holy Roman Church, Henry archbishop of Dublin, William bishop of London, Peter bishop of Winchester, Jocelin bishop of Bath and Glastonbury, Hugh bishop of Lincoln, Walter bishop of Coventry, Benedict bishop of Rochester, Master Pandulf subdeacon and member of the papal household, Brother Aymeric master of the knighthood of the Temple in England, William Marshal earl of Pembroke, William earl of Salisbury, William earl of Warren, William earl of Arundel, Alan de Galloway constable of Scotland, Warin Fitz Gerald, Peter Fitz Herbert, Hubert de Burgh seneschal of Poitou, Hugh de Neville, Matthew Fitz Herbert, Thomas Basset, Alan Basset, Philip Daubeny, Robert de Roppeley, John Marshal, John Fitz Hugh, and other loyal subjects:

(1) FIRST, THAT WE HAVE GRANTED TO GOD, and by this present charter have confirmed for us and our heirs in perpetuity, that the

English Church shall be free, and shall have its rights undiminished, and its liberties unimpaired. That we wish this so to be observed, appears from the fact that of our own free will, before the outbreak of the present dispute between us and our barons, we granted and confirmed by charter the freedom of the Church's elections—a right reckoned to be of the greatest necessity and importance to it—and caused this to be confirmed by Pope Innocent III. This freedom we shall observe ourselves, and desire to be observed in good faith by our heirs in perpetuity.

To ALL FREE MEN OF OUR KINGDOM we have also granted, for us and our heirs for ever, all the liberties written out below, to have and to keep for them and their heirs, of us and our heirs:

(2)   If any earl, baron, or other person that holds lands directly of the Crown, for military service, shall die, and at his death his heir shall be of full age and owe a 'relief', the heir shall have his inheritance on payment of the ancient scale of 'relief'. That is to say, the heir or heirs of an earl shall pay £100 for the entire earl's barony, the heir or heirs of a knight 100s. at most for the entire knight's 'fee', and any man that owes less shall pay less, in accordance with the ancient usage of 'fees'.

(3)   But if the heir of such a person is under age and a ward, when he comes of age he shall have his inheritance without 'relief' or fine.

(4)   The guardian of the land of an heir who is under age shall take from it only reasonable revenues, customary dues, and feudal services. He shall do this without destruction or damage to men or property. If we have given the guardianship of the land to a sheriff, or to any person answerable to us for the revenues, and he commits destruction or damage, we will exact compensation from him, and the land shall be entrusted to two worthy and prudent men of the same 'fee', who shall be answerable to us for the revenues, or to the person to whom we have assigned them. If we have given or sold to anyone the guardianship of such land, and he causes destruction or damage, he shall lose the guardianship of it, and it shall be handed over to two worthy and prudent men of the same 'fee', who shall be similarly answerable to us.

(5) For so long as a guardian has guardianship of such land, he shall maintain the houses, parks, fish preserves, ponds, mills, and everything else pertaining to it, from the revenues of the land itself. When the heir comes of age, he shall restore the whole land to him, stocked with plough teams and such implements of husbandry as the season demands and the revenues from the land can reasonably bear.

(6) Heirs may be given in marriage, but not to someone of lower social standing. Before a marriage takes place, it shall be made known to the heir's next-of-kin.

(7) At her husband's death, a widow may have her marriage portion and inheritance at once and without trouble. She shall pay nothing for her dower, marriage portion, or any inheritance that she and her husband held jointly on the day of his death. She may remain in her husband's house for forty days after his death, and within this period her dower shall be assigned to her.

(8) No widow shall be compelled to marry, so long as she wishes to remain without a husband. But she must give security that she will not marry without royal consent, if she holds her lands of the Crown, or without the consent of whatever other lord she may hold them of.

(9) Neither we nor our officials will seize any land or rent in payment of a debt, so long as the debtor has movable goods sufficient to discharge the debt. A debtor's sureties shall not be distrained upon so long as the debtor himself can discharge his debt. If, for lack of means, the debtor is unable to discharge his debt, his sureties shall be answerable for it. If they so desire, they may have the debtor's lands and rents until they have received satisfaction for the debt that they paid for him, unless the debtor can show that he has settled his obligations to them.

(10) If anyone who has borrowed a sum of money from Jews dies before the debt has been repaid, his heir shall pay no interest on the debt for so long as he remains under age, irrespective of whom he holds his lands. If such a debt falls into the hands of the Crown, it will take nothing except the principal sum specified in the bond.

(11) If a man dies owing money to Jews, his wife may have her

dower and pay nothing towards the debt from it. If he leaves children that are under age, their needs may also be provided for on a scale appropriate to the size of his holding of lands. The debt is to be paid out of the residue, reserving the service due to his feudal lords. Debts owed to persons other than Jews are to be dealt with similarly.

(12) No 'scutage' or 'aid' may be levied in our kingdom without its general consent, unless it is for the ransom of our person, to make our eldest son a knight, and (once) to marry our eldest daughter. For these purposes only a reasonable 'aid' may be levied. 'Aids' from the city of London are to be treated similarly.

(13) The city of London shall enjoy all its ancient liberties and free customs, both by land and by water. We also will and grant that all other cities, boroughs, towns, and ports shall enjoy all their liberties and free customs.

(14) To obtain the general consent of the realm for the assessment of an 'aid'—except in the three cases specified above—or a 'scutage', we will cause the archbishops, bishops, abbots, earls, and greater barons to be summoned individually by letter. To those who hold lands directly of us we will cause a general summons to be issued, through the sheriffs and other officials, to come together on a fixed day (of which at least forty days notice shall be given) and at a fixed place. In all letters of summons, the cause of the summons will be stated. When a summons has been issued, the business appointed for the day shall go forward in accordance with the resolution of those present, even if not all those who were summoned have appeared.

(15) In future we will allow no one to levy an 'aid' from his free men, except to ransom his person, to make his eldest son a knight, and (once) to marry his eldest daughter. For these purposes only a reasonable 'aid' may be levied.

(16) No man shall be forced to perform more service for a knight's 'fee', or other free holding of land, than is due from it.

(17) Ordinary lawsuits shall not follow the royal court around, but shall be held in a fixed place.

(18) Inquests of *novel disseisin, mort d'ancestor,* and *darrein pre-*

*sentment* shall be taken only in their proper county court. We ourselves, or in our absence abroad our chief justice, will send two justices to each county four times a year, and these justices, with four knights of the county elected by the county itself, shall hold the assizes in the county court, on the day and in the place where the court meets.

(19) If any assizes cannot be taken on the day of the county court, as many knights and freeholders shall afterwards remain behind, of those who have attended the court, as will suffice for the administration of justice, having regard to the volume of business to be done.

(20) For a trivial offence, a free man shall be fined only in proportion to the degree of his offence, and for a serious offence correspondingly, but not so heavily as to deprive him of his livelihood. In the same way, a merchant shall be spared his merchandise, and a husbandman the implements of his husbandry, if they fall upon the mercy of a royal court. None of these fines shall be imposed except by the assessment on oath of reputable men of the neighbourhood.

(21) Earls and barons shall be fined only by their equals, and in proportion to the gravity of their offence.

(22) A fine imposed upon the lay property of a clerk in holy orders shall be assessed upon the same principles, without reference to the value of his ecclesiastical benefice.

(23) No town or person shall be forced to build bridges over rivers except those with an ancient obligation to do so.

(24) No sheriff, constable, coroners, or other royal officials are to hold lawsuits that should be held by the royal justices.

(25) Every county, hundred, wapentake, and tithing shall remain at its ancient rent, without increase, except the royal demesne manors.

(26) If at the death of a man who holds a lay 'fee' of the Crown, a sheriff or royal official produces royal letters patent of summons for a debt due to the Crown, it shall be lawful for them to seize and list movable goods found in the lay 'fee' of the dead man to the value of the debt, as assessed by worthy men. Nothing shall be removed until the whole debt is paid, when the residue shall be given

over to the executors to carry out the dead man's will. If no debt is due to the Crown, all the movable goods shall be regarded as the property of the dead man, except the reasonable shares of his wife and children.

(27) If a free man dies intestate, his movable goods are to be distributed by his next-of-kin and friends, under the supervision of the Church. The rights of his debtors are to be preserved.

(28) No constable or other royal official shall take corn or other movable goods from any man without immediate payment, unless the seller voluntarily offers postponement of this.

(29) No constable may compel a knight to pay money for castle-guard if the knight is willing to undertake the guard in person, or with reasonable excuse to supply some other fit man to do it. A knight taken or sent on military service shall be excused from castle-guard for the period of this service.

(30) No sheriff, royal official, or other person shall take horses or carts for transport from any free man, without his consent.

(31) Neither we nor any royal official will take wood for our castle, or for any other purpose, without the consent of the owner.

(32) We will not keep the lands of people convicted of felony in our hand for longer than a year and a day, after which they shall be returned to the lords of the 'fees' concerned.

(33) All fish-weirs shall be removed from the Thames, the Medway, and throughout the whole of England, except on the sea coast.

(34) The writ called *precipe* shall not in future be issued to anyone in respect of any holding of land, if a free man could thereby be deprived of the right of trial in his own lord's court.

(35) There shall be standard measures of wine, ale, and corn (the London quarter), throughout the kingdom. There shall also be a standard width of dyed cloth, russett, and haberject, namely two ells within the selvedges. Weights are to be standardised similarly.

(36) In future nothing shall be paid or accepted for the issue of a writ of inquisition of life or limbs. It shall be given *gratis,* and not refused.

(37) If a man holds land of the Crown by 'fee-farm', 'socage', or 'burgage', and also holds land of someone else for knight's service, we will not have guardianship of his heir, nor of the land that belongs to the other person's 'fee', by virtue of the 'fee-farm', 'socage', or 'burgage', unless the 'fee-farm' owes knight's service. We will not have the guardianship of a man's heir, or of land that he holds of someone else, by reason of any small property that he may hold of the Crown for a service of knives, arrows, or the like.

(38) In future no official shall place a man on trial upon his own unsupported statement, without producing credible witnesses to the truth of it.

(39) No free man shall be seized or imprisoned, or stripped of his rights or possessions, or outlawed or exiled, or deprived of his standing in any other way, nor will we proceed with force against him, or send others to do so, except by the lawful judgement of his equals or by the law of the land.

(40) To no one will we sell, to no one deny or delay right or justice.

(41) All merchants may enter or leave England unharmed and without fear, and may stay or travel within it, by land or water, for purposes of trade, free from all illegal exactions, in accordance with ancient and lawful customs. This, however, does not apply in time of war to merchants from a country that is at war with us. Any such merchants found in our country at the outbreak of war shall be detained without injury to their persons or property, until we or our chief justice have discovered how our own merchants are being treated in the country at war with us. If our own merchants are safe they shall be safe too.

(42) In future it shall be lawful for any man to leave and return to our kingdom unharmed and without fear, by land or water, preserving his allegiance to us, except in time of war, for some short period, for the common benefit of the realm. People that have been imprisoned or outlawed in accordance with the law of the land, people from a country that is at war with us, and merchants—who shall be dealt with as stated above—are excepted from this provision.

(43) If a man holds lands of any 'escheat' such as the 'honour' of Wallingford, Nottingham, Boulogne, Lancaster, or of other 'escheats' in our hand that are baronies, at his death his heir shall give us only the 'relief' and service that he would have made to the baron, had the barony been in the baron's hand. We will hold the 'escheat' in the same manner as the baron held it.

(44) People who live outside the forest need not in future appear before the royal justices of the forest in answer to general summonses, unless they are actually involved in proceedings or are sureties for someone who has been seized for a forest offence.

(45) We will appoint as justices, constables, sheriffs, or other officials, only men that know the law of the realm and are minded to keep it well.

(46) All barons who have founded abbeys, and have charters of English kings or ancient tenure as evidence of this, may have guardianship of them when there is no abbot, as is their due.

(47) All forests that have been created in our reign shall at once be disafforested. River-banks that have been enclosed in our reign shall be treated similarly.

(48) All evil customs relating to forests and warrens, foresters, warreners, sheriffs and their servants, or river-banks and their wardens, are at once to be investigated in every county by twelve sworn knights of the county, and within forty days of their enquiry the evil customs are to be abolished completely and irrevocably. But we, or our chief justice if we are not in England, are first to be informed.

(49) We will at once return all hostages and charters delivered up to us by Englishmen as security for peace or for loyal service.

(50) We will remove completely from their offices the kinsmen of Gerard de Athée, and in future they shall hold no offices in England. The people in question are Engelard de Cigogné, Peter, Guy, and Andrew de Chanceaux, Guy de Cigogné, Geoffrey de Martigny and his brothers, Philip Marc and his brothers, with Geoffrey his nephew, and all their followers.

(51) As soon as peace is restored, we will remove from the king-

dom all the foreign knights, bowmen, their attendants, and the mercenaries that have come to it, to its harm, with horses and arms. (52) To any man whom we have deprived or dispossessed of lands, castles, liberties, or rights, without the lawful judgement of his equals, we will at once restore these. In cases of dispute the matter shall be resolved by the judgement of the twenty-five barons referred to below in the clause for securing the peace [§ 61]. In cases, however, where a man was deprived or dispossessed of something without the lawful judgement of his equals by our father King Henry or our brother King Richard, and it remains in our hands or is held by others under our warranty, we shall have respite for the period commonly allowed to Crusaders, unless a lawsuit had been begun, or an enquiry had been made at our order, before we took the Cross as a Crusader. On our return from the Crusade, or if we abandon it, we will at once render justice in full.

(53) We shall have similar respite in rendering justice in connexion with forests that are to be disafforested, or to remain forests, when these were first afforested by our father Henry or our brother Richard; with the guardianship of lands in another person's 'fee', when we have hitherto had this by virtue of a 'fee' held of us for knight's service by a third party; and with abbeys founded in another person's 'fee', in which the lord of the 'fee' claims to own a right. On our return from the Crusade, or if we abandon it, we will at once do full justice to complaints about these matters.

(54) No one shall be arrested or imprisoned on the appeal of a woman for the death of any person except her husband.

(55) All fines that have been given to us unjustly and against the law of the land, and all fines that we have exacted unjustly, shall be entirely remitted or the matter decided by a majority judgement of the twenty-five barons referred to below in the clause for securing the peace [§ 61] together with Stephen, archbishop of Canterbury, if he can be present, and such others as he wishes to bring with him. If the archbishop cannot be present, proceedings shall continue without him, provided that if any of the twenty-five barons has been involved in a similar suit himself, his judgement shall be set

aside, and someone else chosen and sworn in his place, as a substitute for the single occasion, by the rest of the twenty-five.

(56) If we have deprived or dispossessed any Welshmen of lands, liberties, or anything else in England or in Wales, without the lawful judgement of their equals, these are at once to be returned to them. A dispute on this point shall be determined in the Marches by the judgement of equals. English law shall apply to holdings of land in England, Welsh law to those in Wales, and the law of the Marches to those in the Marches. The Welsh shall treat us and ours in the same way.

(57) In cases where a Welshman was deprived or dispossessed of anything, without the lawful judgement of his equals, by our father King Henry or our brother King Richard, and it remains in our hands or is held by others under our warranty, we shall have respite for the period commonly allowed to Crusaders, unless a lawsuit had been begun, or an enquiry had been made at our order, before we took the Cross as a Crusader. But on our return from the Crusade, or if we abandon it, we will at once do full justice according to the laws of Wales and the said regions.

(58) We will at once return the son of Llywelyn, all Welsh hostages, and the charters delivered to us as security for the peace.

(59) With regard to the return of the sisters and hostages of Alexander, king of Scotland, his liberties and his rights, we will treat him in the same way as our other barons of England, unless it appears from the charters that we hold from his father William, formerly king of Scotland, that he should be treated otherwise. This matter shall be resolved by the judgement of his equals in our court.

(60) All these customs and liberties that we have granted shall be observed in our kingdom in so far as concerns our own relations with our subjects. Let all men of our kingdom, whether clergy or laymen, observe them similarly in their relations with their own men.

(61) SINCE WE HAVE GRANTED ALL THESE THINGS for God, for the better ordering of our kingdom, and to allay the discord that has arisen between us and our barons, and since we desire that they

shall be enjoyed in their entirety, with lasting strength, for ever, we give and grant to the barons the following security:

The barons shall elect twenty-five of their number to keep, and cause to be observed with all their might, the peace and liberties granted and confirmed to them by this charter.

If we, our chief justice, our officials, or any of our servants offend in any respect against any man, or transgress any of the articles of the peace or of this security, and the offence is made known to four of the said twenty-five barons, they shall come to us—or in our absence from the kingdom to the chief justice—to declare it and claim immediate redress. If we, or in our absence abroad the chief justice, make no redress within forty days, reckoning from the day on which the offence was declared to us or to him, the four barons shall refer the matter to the rest of the twenty-five barons, who may distrain upon and assail us in every way possible, with the support of the whole community of the land, by seizing our castles, lands, possessions, or anything else saving only our own person and those of the queen and our children, until they have secured such redress as they have determined upon. Having secured the redress, they may then resume their normal obedience to us.

Any man who so desires may take an oath to obey the commands of the twenty-five barons for the achievement of these ends, and to join with them in assailing us to the utmost of his power. We give public and free permission to take this oath to any man who so desires, and at no time will we prohibit any man from taking it. Indeed, we will compel any of our subjects who are unwilling to take it to swear it at our command.

If one of the twenty-five barons dies or leaves the country, or is prevented in any other way from discharging his duties, the rest of them shall choose another baron in his place, at their discretion, who shall be duly sworn in as they were.

In the event of disagreement among the twenty-five barons on any matter referred to them for decision, the verdict of the majority present shall have the same validity as a unanimous verdict of the whole twenty-five, whether these were all present or some of those summoned were unwilling or unable to appear.

The twenty-five barons shall swear to obey all the above articles faithfully, and shall cause them to be obeyed by others to the best of their power.

We will not seek to procure from anyone, either by our own efforts or those of a third party, anything by which any part of these concessions or liberties might be revoked or diminished. Should such a thing be procured, it shall be null and void and we will at no time make use of it, either ourselves or through a third party.

(62) We have remitted and pardoned fully to all men any ill-will, hurt, or grudges that have arisen between us and our subjects, whether clergy or laymen, since the beginning of the dispute. We have in addition remitted fully, and for our own part have also pardoned, to all clergy and laymen any offences committed as a result of the said dispute between Easter in the sixteenth year of our reign [i.e. 1215] and the restoration of peace.

In addition we have caused letters patent to be made for the barons, bearing witness to this security and to the concessions set out above, over the seals of Stephen archbishop of Canterbury, Henry archbishop of Dublin, the other bishops named above, and Master Pandulf.

(63) IT IS ACCORDINGLY OUR WISH AND COMMAND that the English Church shall be free, and that men in our kingdom shall have and keep all these liberties, rights, and concessions, well and peaceably in their fulness and entirety for them and their heirs, of us and our heirs, in all things and all places for ever.

Both we and the barons have sworn that all this shall be observed in good faith and without deceit. Witness the abovementioned people and many others.

Given by our hand in the meadow that is called Runnymede, between Windsor and Staines, on the fifteenth day of June in the seventeenth year of our reign [i.e. 1215: *the new regnal year began on 28 May*].

## Table I

# Sovereigns of England From the Conquest to the "Glorious Revolution"

| NAME | REIGN |
|------|-------|
| **THE NORMANS** | |
| William I | 1066–1087 |
| William II | 1087–1100 |
| Henry I | 1100–1135 |
| Stephen | 1135–1154* |
| **PLANTAGENETS (ANGEVINS)** | |
| Henry II | 1154–1189 |
| Richard I | 1189–1199 |
| John | 1199–1216 |
| Henry III | 1216–1272 |
| Edward I | 1272–1307 |
| Edward II | 1307–1327 |
| Edward III | 1327–1377 |
| Richard II | 1377–1399 |
| **LANCASTRIANS†** | |
| Henry IV | 1399–1413 |
| Henry V | 1413–1422 |
| Henry VI | 1422–1461 |
| **YORKISTS†** | |
| Edward IV | 1461–1483 |
| Edward V | 1483 |

| NAME | REIGN |
|------|-------|
| Richard III | 1483–1485 |

### TUDORS

| | |
|------|-------|
| Henry VII | 1485–1509 |
| Henry VIII | 1509–1547 |
| Edward VI | 1547–1553 |
| Mary I | 1553–1554 |
| Philip and Mary | 1554–1558 |
| Elizabeth I | 1558–1603 |

### STUARTS

| | |
|------|-------|
| James I# | 1603–1625 |
| Charles I | 1625–1649 |

### REVOLUTIONARY ERA

| | |
|------|-------|
| The Commonwealth | 1649–1660\*\* |
| The Protectorate | 1653–1660\*\* |

### STUARTS

| | |
|------|-------|
| Charles II | 1660–1685 |
| James II | 1685–1688 |

### REVOLUTION OF 1688

| | |
|------|-------|
| William and Mary | 1689–1702‡ |

\*Deposed, March-December, 1141
†"Wars of the Roses"
#James VI of Scotland
\*\*Most of the so-called Commonwealth was under the "Lords Protector," Oliver Cromwell (1653–1658) and his son Richard
‡First constitutional monarchs under Bill of Rights (Table II)

## Table II

# Selected Documents of English Constitutional Development

1100 *Coronation Charter* (HENRY I)
Promise to "observe good laws" and reform a specified list of "bad laws"

1215 *Magna Carta* (JOHN)
Original agreement between the King and the barons

1216 *Magna Carta* (HENRY III)
First reissue by advisers of the King during his minority

1217 *Magna Carta* (HENRY III)
*Carta de Foresta* (HENRY III)
Division of "charter of general liberties" from separate charter of forest laws

1225 *Magna Carta* (HENRY III)
*Carta de Foresta* (HENRY III)
Definitive reissue of the charters on Henry's majority

1267 *Statute of Marlborough* (HENRY III)
Elaboration of feudal law principles developed subsequent to the "great charters"

1275 *Statute of Westminster I* (EDWARD I)
First of great constitutional statutes of Edward, further elaborating on principles of feudal law

1278 *Statute of Gloucester* (EDWARD I)
Another of Edward's constitutional statutes, famous for its rule against waste of land and resources

1285 *Statute of Westminster II* (EDWARD I)
Known primarily for its opening chapter entitled, *De*

*Donis,* an attempted reform in the feudal law on inheritances

1290 *Statute "Quia Emptores"* (EDWARD I)
An attempted limitation on subinfeudation to prevent dissipation of services owing the grantor of the estate

1290 *Statute "Quo Warranto"* (EDWARD I)
A fixing of "the beginning of legal memory" for proof of grants of rights; for easy reference, and because it marked the farthest backward extent of readily available records, the coronation date of Richard I—September 3, 1189—was used

1297 *Confirmatio Cartarum* (EDWARD I)
This "confirmation of the charters" of 1225 was the first of many reassertions of the continuing validity of Magna Carta, first by Kings and later by Parliaments, until it became universally assumed that the Great Charter was the first principle of the English constitution

1300 *Articuli super Cartas* (EDWARD I)
The "articles on the charters" were, in effect, amendments to this constitutional document; they actually were further elaborations of the feudal law like the other great statutes under Edward

1352 *"Statute V"* (EDWARD III)
Although it had no generic title, this statute elaborated on the famous Chapter 39 (29 in the reissue) on the matter of due process of law and trial before one's peers

1628 *Petition of Right* (CHARLES I)
The beginning of the modern constitution of England dates from this document, which among other things perpetuated the due process guarantee of Chapter 39 (29) of Magna Carta

TABLE II 147

1679 *Habeas Corpus Act* (CHARLES II)
A guarantee of the writ of *habeas corpus* in its modern meaning as a protection against unreasonable detention before trial

1689 *Bill of Rights* (WILLIAM III and MARY II)
The forerunner of the American Bill of Rights, the guarantees in this document were accepted by William of Orange and his wife as conditions of their own coronation

1701 *Act of Settlement* (WILLIAM III)
This statute, defining the conditions under which future monarchs should succeed to the throne, completed the development of the constitutional monarchy

# Suggested Books
# for Further Reading

In 1965, on the 750th anniversary of the original drafting of Magna Carta, a series of booklets on the history and present-day significance of the Great Charter was published by the Virginia Magna Carta Commission. These booklets, intended for high school, college and general readers alike, may be obtained from the University Press of Virginia, Box 3608, University Station, Charlottesville, Virginia 22903. They include the following:

Maurice Ashley, *Magna Carta in the Seventeenth Century*

John E. Bebout, *An Ancient Partnership: Local Government, Magna Carta, National Interest*

Gottfried Dietze, *Magna Carta and Property*

Arthur Goodhart, *The Law of the Land*

J. C. Holt, *The Making of Magna Carta*

Yale Kamisar, Fred E. Inbau and Thurman Arnold, *Criminal Justice in Our Time*

Daniel J. Meador, *Habeas Corpus and Magna Carta: Dualism of Power and Liberty*

Doris M. Stenton, *After Runnymede: Magna Carta in the Middle Ages*

Arthur E. Sutherland, *The Church Shall be Free: A Glimpse at Eight Centuries of Church and State*

# Index

# A Note About the Author

William F. Swindler, lawyer, historian and educator began his writing career as a newspaper man. For more than thirty years he has been an avid student of English and American constitutional history and is now acknowledged an outstanding authority on the subject. He is currently professor of law at the Marshall-Wythe School of Law of the College of William and Mary.